J.L. Hudson's Department Store,
downtown Detroit. 1998

Urban Ecology
Detroit and Beyond

Editor: Kyong Park/ International Center for Urban Ecology [iCUE]

Book design: Matthias Rick
Cover design: MAP Office
Associate editor: Tamalyn Miller
Preliminary design and editing: Manuela Tromben
Research: Toni Moceri
Image process: Sebastian Holtmann, David Cardenas

All photographs are by Kyong Park, unless noted otherwise

First published 2005 by
MAP BOOK PUBLISHERS
5th Floor, 231, Wing Lok Street
Sheung Wan, Hong Kong
www.map-office.com

Available in Europe through IDEA BOOKS
Available in North, South and Central America through D.A.P. / Distributed Art Publishers Inc.

ISBN 96286040-4-X
Printed in Hong Kong, 2005

This book is made possible in part by the generous support of the Graham Foundation for Advanced Studies in the Fine Arts.

A project of International Center for Urban Ecology [iCUE]
Detroit/New York/Berlin
In association with StoreFront for Art and Architecture
New York

Urban Ecology

Detroit and Beyond

Kyong Park/iCUE

Dedicated to
Cyrus and Shirin

MAP BOOK PUBLISHERS

Urban Ecology: Detroit and Beyond is a journey through different cities, encountering their cinematic landscapes, colors, and textures, where past and future mix. I began this journey at StoreFront for Art and Architecture in New York, with persuasive exhibitions like *The New American Ghetto* by Camilo José Vergara, *Beirut* by Gabriele Basilico, (curated by Francesco Bonomi), and *Warchitecture* by the Association of Architects of Bosnia and Herzegovina. These and other projects demonstrated that architecture and cities are not just commodities to be used and discarded. They are also spatial and temporal territories of identities and relations between cultures, and thus the most essential record of how we evolve and fail at the same time.

I moved to Detroit in 1998 to collaborate with Stephen P. Vogel, the dean of the School of Architecture at the University of Detroit Mercy, and Peter Lynch, then director of the Architecture Program at the Cranbrook Academy of Art, to develop a project for converting an old Packard plant into a facility to mass produce manufactured homes. This idea made sense for Detroit, with its abundance of unemployed, unskilled labor and obsolete industry. We planned to award the first line of assembled houses free to those who made them so they could resettle the vacant land that surrounds the Packard plant. The project was never realized, however. Instead, a number of meetings with extraordinary, resilient residents was to reshape my thinking and my approach to the city of Detroit.

Lee Burns, a retired engineer from Cleveland, moved to Concord Street, right next to the Packard plant. He envisioned a new beginning emanating from the empty spaces and buildings, and inspired my students from SCI-ARC in Los Angeles and me as we sat in his backyard listening to him describe how he dug the ground five feet deep all around a dying tree, and filled the trench with new soil and nutrients, so that the tree now shaded us all. Shortly afterwards, Andrew Zago moved back to Detroit, imagining that new architecture could be made here where a new city should be built.

Then I met Paul Weertz, perhaps the most unusual high school science teacher around. He had turned about three acres of the yard of Catherine Ferguson High School into a farm, and was teaching several hundred young mothers about responsibility, commitment, and self sufficiency by showing them how care for horses, goats, sheep, and chickens, and how to plant trees, vegetables,

Preface

Kyong Park

and herbs. He rented me a house on Farnsworth Street, where he lives, and which he has preserved as one of very few residential blocks in the near eastside with most of the houses still standing and occupied. He bought houses that people left behind, and then fixed them to rent or sell to those who wanted to build a new community with him. He was a genuine urban pioneer.

The *Heidelberg Project* by Tyree Guyton and Jenenne Whitfield was only a mile from there. They had transformed a dead street with magical objects—hundreds of vacuum cleaners, dolls, signs, car hoods, shoes and other abandoned odds and ends that they painted and attached to trees and houses; the most domestic urban monument you will ever see.

Eventually the journey lead me to Field Street, where Grace Lee Boggs has lived fifty of her ninety years and graced so many people in this die-hard city of activism. Once I became a friend of her vision, I was welcomed by Shea Howell of Detroit Summer, Jim Embry of the Boggs Center, Scott Kurashige and others who are trying to bring back Chinatown from extinction, Elena Herrada of the Committee for Political Resurrection (CPR) who is attempting to alter perhaps the most corrupt system of representation in the nation, and Charles Simmons who moved back to the family house where he grew up to try to rebuild the block as it once was.

It was after meeting these and other remarkable individuals, that I choose not to work on the site, or the source, of Detroit's decline, but rather to focus on the building of a new city, together with those who had already started the process. So, with Andrew Zago and Stephen Vogel, I set up the International Center for Urban Ecology [iCUE] in 1998.

And some help came from outside: Craig Bachellier, Pilar Ortiz, Francisca Benitez, Tony Hamboussi, and most importantly Manuela Tromben from New York came to collaborate on iCUE workshops; Hannes Brunner brought his great students from Kiel, Germany; Gill Doran paid a visit from London; and Charles Waldheim from Chicago; Deborah Grotfledt and Rick Lowe from Project Row House in Houston; Mel Chin and Linda Larsen from North Carolina; Renee Greene, Meg Webster, and Andrej Vovk from New York; Mark Anderson from Seattle; and Tricia Ward from Los Angeles all enriched the *Architecture of Resistance*.

A view of Woodraw Wilson Avenue, Lincoln Avenue, and Auberndale Avenue (from left), at the northwest corner of Davidson Freeway (in view at far left and right) and Lodge Freeway, Detroit. 2003

Chris Pomodoro is thanked for producing the video documentation of *Adamah: A New Equity for Detroit*, a project from a collective design studio at the University of Detroit Mercy, which I taught together with Stephen Vogel; Daniel Pitera and Andrew Sturm of Detroit Collaborative Design Studio for collaborating with me on the "fugitive" 24260; and Anita Vogel for finding the "original" 24260. I am also indebted to Jim Cope who invited his friends and community to be interviewed for *Old House/New House*.

Then I started to "export" Detroit, with 24260 first going to Orléans, thanks to *Archilab* and Frédéric Migayrou, Béatrice Simonot and Marie-ange Brayer. In Sindelfingen, Konrad and Ingrid Burgbacher provided a perfect empty lot for it to sit on outside, and in Karlsruhe, Angelika Stepken secured a beautiful space for it inside. Thanks also go to Lily van Ginneken and Jan Wijle in the Hague for storing 24260 for more than a year, and to Ronald Van Tienhoven and Boris Gerrets for making a documentary about 24260 and the people of Detroit.

I thank Philip Oswalt for inviting me to participate in the *Project Shrinking Cities*, and giving me a marvelous chance to see Ivanovo, Liverpool, Manchester, Halle, and Leipzig over and over. I learned about these cities from Sergei Sitar, Alexander Sverdlov, Mitch Cope, Philipp Misselwitz, Joshua Bolchover and Paul Domela. Thanks go to the superbly organized staff of *Project Shrinking Cities* in Berlin, especially Anke Hagemann and Elke Beyer, while Christiane Mennicke, and Torsten Birne allowed me to project *BAR/GDR/FRG* inside a giant construction hole; Johannes Köhler for breaking into buildings, climbing containers, and freezing under the sweeping wind of the Elbe River to get insanely slow pan shots; Thilo Fröbel for his most gentle walks with me to edit Dresden; Leo Fitzmorris for taking me to Norris Green in Liverpool; Evgeniy Shmelev for perfect translations while Victor, the taxi driver took me to very special places in Ivanovo and even all the way to the Moscow airport; Benjamin Foerster-Baldenius, Matthias Rick, and Cora Hegewald for tasting my pseudo-Korean cooking in an empty Chinese restaurant in Halle

An open sunday church at the southwest corner of Chene and Frederick, Detroit. 2003

Neustadt. Further, I appreciate Marco Brizzi for premiering *Detroit: Making It Better for You* in Florence, and Diana Baldon and Emily Pethick of Cubitt in London for the same reason.

Recently, I had the incredible opportunity to tour ten cities of the western Balkans, from Ljubjana to Tirana, with Marjetica Potrč , to meet Stevan Vukovic and Ivan Kucina in Belgrade, Srdjan Jovanovic Weiss in Novi Sad, Azra Aksamija in Sarajevo, Sean Snyder in Skopje, and countless other artists, architects, sociologists, philosophers, curators and others, across the mountains of Kosovo and along the Danube River. Modernist architecture there is more vibrant and diverse than in other socialist territories, and these physical memorials of a once idealized attempt for human emancipation within a shared society are now being hybridized by informal urbanism under the influence of unabashed capitalism to produce "wild cities."

For the book, I thank Michael Bell, James Wines, and William Menking for supporting this book; Toni Moceri for much needed research; Manuela Tromben for her tireless challenge to my thoughts while organizing the materials in this book; Matthias Rick for miraculously giving clarity and order to these complex and diverse contents; Tamalyn Miller for sharp, thoughtful, and creative editing; Peter Lang for critical guidance; and Laurent Gutierrez and Valérie Portefaix for being so wonderfully open as publishers.

But these pages would not have been inked without generous support from the Graham Foundation for Advanced Studies in the Fine Arts, and the projects were made possible with support from the McMartha Fund; The Rockefeller Foundation; the Andy Warhol Foundation; the Stephen A. and Diana L. Goldberg Foundation; the University of Detroit Mercy, School of Architecture; The National Endowment for the Arts; Kulturstiftung des Bundes (German Federal Cultural Foundation) and many others.

But the most important believers in this nomadic laboratory for future cities were Stephen Vogel, who seemed to be amused with my rebellious behaviors, and Martha Wilson who has, like me, an affinity for impossible projects.

1

Over My Dead City

Peter Lang

Not in a very long time has the architectural subject become so loaded with tragic meaning or so overcharged with symbolic weight. The felling of the World Trade Towers (a reemergent ritual from the early Middle Ages), or the unsubtle attributions of defiance and memory enshrouding the replacement project (a 1776-foot-high bully pulpit) demonstrate the inherent fragility and dubious expressiveness of the architectural corpus post 9/11. In this new epic of Wagnerian histrionics what else is to be expected of architecture but armored buildings and exaggerated moral proclamations in the face of unequivocal acts of hatred and political defiance?

It's no longer possible to formulate a redemptive architecture *tout court*. Rather, the present crisis necessitates much more radical responses that would be more capable of transcending the limitations of the autonomously generated architectural element. How else to begin than by returning to the subject of the city, in order to reexamine the incredibly altered condition of the present urban landscape as it is shaped by an economically-fragmented socially-heterogeneous global society.[1]

The city, if this term is still to hold any meaning, should be considered a vibrant manifestation of intense constructive and destructive energies, released from centric poles or linear alignments. The new urban conglomerations behave unpredictably, flipping rapidly from congested to decongested states, stretching perimeters, dropping centers, defying any of the standard formulas underlining the late modern rules of urban determinacy.

Actually, today's contemporary concrete and wire lace is really not a city at all, but an amorphously spreading construction site whose identity derives not from what is achieved but from what is changing. The city becomes a metabolic work-in-progress that spills through space and time, chaotically reorganizing itself as it responds to an infinite number of economic and social pressures. This might be the most significant lesson today, amply demonstrated in Asia, where the shear rapidity of growth and demolition, expansion and abandonment, has made permanence an almost valueless currency.[2]

Kyong Park's uniquely conceived work on urban ecologies suggests a much broader approach to the city than might first be inferred, considering that the term ecology is largely assumed to deal only with green or sustainability practices. As such his research stands at the intersection of what is decisively becoming a new discipline, and is significantly the first urban case study to be put to press in this new series *Guidelines*.

Representing the bridge between distinct artistic and urban currents, Park's project has brought new and reinvigorated focus to the contemporary city. His poetic peeling back of Detroit's scarred past to reveal its bucolic but tragic destiny is an exercise inspired not from mainstream academia but from a subversive counter-tendency involving artists, artist collectives, curators, cross-disciplinary researchers, writers, film directors, and disillusioned professionals all hot-wired together into an expansive global network.

1 In his critique on the European cultural "rift" between Expressionism and the Neue Sachlichkeit, Manfredo Tafuri observed: "Between the destruction of the object, its replacement by process intended to be experienced as such (a transformation effected by the artistic revolution brought about by the Bauhaus and the Constructivist currents), and the exasperation of the object (typical of the lacerating but ambiguous eclecticism of the Expressionists), there could be no real dialogue." Though Tafuri would ultimately debunk process itself given its links to the early twentieth-century socially constituted state planning, his remarks address a similar predicament confronted by architects today, whereby current technologically-driven expressionists (blobists, membranists, fragmentists) are locked in conflict with urban-derivative systemists (datascapists, mappists, environmentalists). This time around, however, the state is largely absent from the equation. Manfredo Tafuri, "Toward a Critique of Architectural Ideology," originally published in *Contrapiano 1* (January—April 1969) and reprinted in K. Michael Hays, ed., *Architectural Theory since 1968*, trans. Stephan Sartarelli (Cambridge: MIT Press, 1998), 23.

2 Botond Bognar analyzed Tokyo's short building lifecycles, writing: "Tokyo is characterized by its sense of lightness, the rapid cycles of building/demolition, and thus by a high degree of ephemerality." Botond Bognar, "The Ephemeral Metropolis Tokyo as an Informational World City" (paper presented at the ASCA International conference, Istanbul, June 15-19, 2001).

1 The Assembly Building of Bosnia & Herzegovina, Sarajevo (photo: Milomir Kovacevic © 1992)

2 (photo: Kyong Park © 2005)

Park relates to the invisible neighborhoods of inner-city Detroit, just as he is drawn to the forgotten communities surviving in the cities of former East Germany. His aim is not to make something new, however, but to recognize the vital in what is already there. This soft approach to the city, which discounts hard interventions in the name of formulaic improvements and stale market strategies, is if nothing else the effectuation of a highly critical form of urban damage control. But rather than repeat the contents of Park's project here, I prefer to briefly connect a couple dots in an attempt to situate his recent work consisting mainly of research, documentation, and creative interventions within an expanding field of operations that addresses what I have come to consider as an emergent *geocultural* discipline.

In consequence, Park's contribution should not be considered a sole instance or an isolated viewpoint, but instead part of a growing concern among a diverse group of fellow travelers who are acting with great urgency on the city. The odd mix of nationalities and global urban themes within this group found their earliest manifestations in the programs of some of the more prestigious world art venues in the mid '90s. Almost imperceptibly, these institutions, once representing the epitome of the commercial art fair, were gradually infiltrated by a new generation of politicized curators and directors bent on critically confronting the aftereffects of an all-encompassing post-cold war global crisis.

International art exhibitions, along with similarly inspired architecture showcases taking place periodically from city to city, have ultimately succeeded in engaging impressively large transnational audiences, despite mixed receptions. Documenta X in 1997 and XI in 2002 respectively; the Manifesta transient exhibitions based out of Rotterdam beginning in 1996; the Kwangju Korea Biennale in 1997; the Venice Architecture Biennales in Italy, from 2000 on (whatever the extreme fluctuations in curatorial competency responsible for setting the general themes and the independent nature of the national pavilions); as well as a spreading number of international biennales were indispensable in reconfiguring the basic premise of the international exhibition platform in relationship to the broader global community and the world city.[3]

Frequently these major annuals and biennials were pinned to a series of critical discussions,

3 The increasing number of similar projects is growing exponentially see: Shrinking Cities *www.shrinkingcities*; Urban Catalysts and Urban Drifts in Berlin; the Biennales in Dakar, Sao Paolo, Istanbul, and Athens to name a few of the more prominent examples.

3 A view of the Palace of People, Bucharest, Romania (photo: Kevin Neel © 1996)

4 Reichstag in reconstruction, Berlin (photo: Stefanie Bürkle © 1995)

5 Havana (photo: courtesy of Carlos Garaicoa, 97 Kwangju Biennale © 1992)

6 Cato Manor, South Africa (photo: courtesy of Ronald Wall and Ewoud Netten/Housing Generator, 97 Kwangju Biennale © 1992)

4 Steven Jacobs, *Shreds of Boring Postcards: Toward a Posturban Aesthetics on the Generic and Everyday*, ed. Post ex sub dis, Ghent Urban Studies Team (Rotterdam: 010 Publishers, 2002), 32.

5 Storefront's experiments in façade modifications culminated in 1993 with the Vito Acconci/Steven Holl hinged façade. See *Acconci, Holl. StoreFront for Art and Architecture*, ed. Edelbert Köb, Arno Ritter, Paul Ott (Hatje Cantz Publishers, 2001).

6 Kyong Park, "Images of the Future: The Architecture of a New Geography," in Kwangju Biennale Foundation, ed., *97 Kwangju Biennale Unmapping the Earth* (Kwangju: Kwangju Biennale Press, 1997), 128.

7 Lee Young-chul, "On 'Unmapping the Earth,'" in Kwangju Biennale Foundation, ed., *97 Kwangju Biennale Unmapping the Earth* (Kwangju: Kwangju Biennale Press, 1997), 35.

6

seminars, and web chat rooms to further identify issues not necessarily associated with the standard creative artistic practice. The international art exhibitions beginning in the mid '90s seem to have dramatically jumped dimensions, grouping within their fold a number of disaffected activists bent on seeking out specific territorial contradictions and social imbalances.

The new breed of multidisciplinary artist is a far more prescient gauge of the dramatic transformations affecting society than his or her more rigidly focused professional counterpart, and clearly serves to instigate a debate on the subject of the contemporary city and its impact on new forms of cultural behavior. As Stevens Jacobs aptly put it, "Now that David Lynch has arguably come to be a more important point of reference for architects and urban planners than Kevin Lynch, it seems high time to cast a more than superficial glance at artistic representations of the contemporary city."[4]

Today's heavily politicized conceptual artists are the indispensable sparks that set all other forces in motion. The mutually beneficial dialogue between individual artists and architects was central to Park's founding vision and direction of StoreFront for Art and Architecture, the alternative gallery that opened in downtown New York in 1982. This synthesis between art and architecture, most emblematically realized in the hinged storefront façade by Vito Acconci/Steven Holl completed in 1993, effectively set the stage for a long series of important collaborative efforts.[5]

StoreFront for Art and Architecture became one of the few American venues open to multidisciplinary projects on the contemporary city. Park instigated and contributed to this growing international tendency. As one of the curators for the international section of the 1997 Kwangju Biennale in Korea and later as a member of the Board of Advisors for the Venice Architecture Biennale in 2000, Park further consolidated his role as urban activist, as he sought to match a wide variety of tactical approaches to the difficult terrains he came to inhabit. As he wrote for the Kwangju exhibition catalogue in 1997, "Although, biennales have traditionally invited artists and their works, I decided to invite cities instead. This was partly to de-emphasize the showcasing of artists as individuals, and I suppose, to a certain degree, the commercialization of the artwork as well. Cities that were at a critical moment in their history were sought, and the artists whose work could best capture them were later found."[6]

Looking back to that particular moment in time when the exhibition took place, the 97 Kwangju Biennale unarguably contributed to shifting public attention squarely on the emerging global city, its new and radical forms of urban culture and the incredibly explosive transformations that were changing the very fabric of daily life. Lee Young-chul, in setting the premise for "Unmapping the Earth," sought to fling wide open the doors to an enhanced reality. Young-chul wrote, "'Unmapping' exists every time, everywhere, from a place where boundary and discrimination are most apparent, to where they are most concealed, from deep human instinct to trivial things, and from the breath of a living body to a cold artificial produce."[7]

The exhibition, which brought together a pantheon of exceptional thinkers, critics, multimedia artists and architects was parceled into a chaos inspired "hybrid" set of living categories. As one of the five elements of this conceptual cartographic project, Kyong Park's prescient assembly of "cities" was in fact a meditative reflection on a dispersed set of troubled urban environments, destabilized neighborhoods, and colossal-scale interventions that posited an unsettling awakening to the city's latest transformations. Clearly, stringing together Gabriele Basilico's *Beirut*; Emmet Gowin's *Jerusalem 1*; Camilo José Vergara's *New American Ghetto*; Hannes Brunner's *Rome Corviale*; and Milomir Kovacevic's *Sarajevo* was itself sufficient to underscore that Park's perspective was not geared to the usual trivia in the art world. [8]

Though not as evident in its urban scope, Catherine David's Documenta X, a five-year investigative project put on exhibition in 1997 in Kassel, Germany, was one of the more renowned of these early anti-art forums to disturb longstanding presumptions on artistic production. As Catherine David remarked in her online forum: "I have often described the Documenta X as a cultural event, presenting contemporary aesthetic practices (the term 'art' is no longer suitable for describing or summarizing the heterogeneous artistic methods of our time) in a manner as diverse as possible and in a variety of facets."[9]

The kind of diversity that Catherine David sought was precisely the kind of multicultural multi-themed assemblage of critical works that broke with the sclerotic individual idol system of the past. Significantly, she introduced a provocative multimedia environment that was intended to mirror the world, however miniature it might have appeared through her stock of thirteen artist teams.[10] The art world's reception to this new breed of global show was mixed to say the least.[11] But for many critics working on the fringes of the architectural and urban disciplines, these important international exhibitions demonstrated very real and applicable methods for dealing with the altogether unprocessed phenomenon of the global city. Such techniques would be further adapted in subsequent venues, combining multidisciplinary research and critical interactive strategies to creatively confront cities, borders, and peripheries as well as to dialogue with the politically oppressed and their emerging methods of social resistance.

8 Other notable participants included Harold Szeemann, Friedrich Kittler, and Lawrence Grossberg, with contributions by Paul Virilio, Slavoj Žižek, and John Rajchman.

9 Catherine David, posted on *www.documenta.de*, June 20, 1997.

10 The organizer of the Johannesburg Biennale and future director of Documenta XI, Okwui Enwezor, a participant in *100 Days 100 Guests* organized by Catherine David back in 1997, faulted the DX for not going far enough. "Having said that, we in Johannesburg have other priorities, and our priorities do not in any way coincide with the ones of exhibitions like Documenta. Even if Catherine David has made great attempts to break apart this incestuous relationship between the market, dealers, institutions and so on, it still remains an astonishingly Western institution and by 'Western' I don't mean that in any kind of derogatory way, it simply means that it is a different kind of spatial practice that exists in that area." From an interview by Pat Binder and Gerhard Haupt, in Universes in Universe, July 5, 1997. web site: *www.universes-in-universe.de/car/africus/e_enwez.htm*.

11 For a particularly blunt appraisal of the rising multicultural trend taking over the art world see Michael Salcman's review of Documenta XI, "German Diary Documenta XI in "Kassel: The Artist as Detective; Knowledge as Art" posted on *www.peekreview.net*, 2002.

12 Detroit is increasingly attracting attention, especially the incredible downtown backdrops in the 2002 film *8 Mile*, directed by Curtis Hanson and starring Eminem. An interesting documentation and workshop was conceived and published in *Stalking Detroit* (no relation to the Rome-based urban research group Stalker), ed. Georgia Daskalakis, Charles Waldheim, and Jason Young (Barcelona: Actar, 2002).

7

8

Park, in the meantime, exchanged roles, seeking to engage the subject of the city directly as an activist and artist rather than as a creative ringleader. His project on Detroit marks a significant turning phase, in which he begins to investigate the complex history of Detroit's decline and grassroots resurgence, taking advantage of the opportunity to observe in real time and real space the mechanism that wracked apart a city of such monumental proportions.[12]

Park's highly significant work presented here should open entire spheres of urban and peripheral-based research not yet thoroughly studied and documented. That he is in good company should be amply evident given the number of prominently active men and women currently engaged in similarly driven urban-based projects included in this volume. But there is much work to be done just to properly flesh out the contours of this emerging discipline.[13]

In the meantime, the great cities around the world continue to slip off their maps as they plunge head-on into new urban unknowns. Like the open cities of a war-torn past, these latest phenomena neither heed to political dogmas nor bend to economic pressures from above. Instead, it is the present city's heterogeneous society itself that continuously renegotiates its claim to persevere and prosper. Might not the education of the architect today, in the broadest sense, become a sort of full-emersion urban therapy?

13 There are of course a whole set of investigative strategies that have acted on the territory of the city and its regions that I don't have space to detail here. I have sought to merely highlight the most important urban-related trends that have impacted on the scene internationally and that were most evidently accessible from the North American side of the Atlantic. The current generation of urban activists emerging in the last decade from northern and southern Europe, the Near East, Asia, and South America have given rise to an incredibly important body of work dealing with the new urban culture.

7 Beirut (photo: Gabriele Basilico © 1991)

8 A proposal for Pudong, Shanghai by Toyo Ito. 1992

9 The City of Muang Thong Thani, Bankok (photo: John Gollings © 1997)

9

Surviving to Create

Stephen Vogel

Detroit is an anomaly among world cities. It is at once a center of manufacturing known worldwide and located at the apex of one of the richest regions in the United States, and simultaneously the ultimate shrinking, post-industrial city. The city has suffered unprecedented devastation, population loss, and disinvestment. This same condition, however, creates an open laboratory for social and physical experimentation that attracts hardy residents, expanding corporations, self-reliant urban pioneers, artists, and musicians. While struggling to keep streetlights working, the city can simultaneously induce General Motors, the largest automobile manufacturing corporation in the world, to invest billions into its new world headquarters and adjoining areas. On the other hand, phantom real estate development "deals" are made daily, only to somehow belie fruition. It is a city of hope and despair; potential and frustration.

As a forty-year resident and professional in the city, I have seen the dichotomy of Detroit at all levels of interaction. The neighborhood in which I reside consists of amazingly affordable, spacious, beautiful homes and diverse, caring urban professional and working-class neighbors. On the other hand, during economic downturns there have been crime sprees, especially the "on order" stealing of automobiles; shopping, by necessity, takes place in the suburbs; the local post office has a history of "disappearing" mail; and our children, again out of necessity, attended private schools. Our daughter's friends, who attended her faith-based suburban private school, were not allowed to visit our home because it is situated south of the "eight mile" divide. She and her friends "snuck out" to partake of the forbidden fruits of the downtown and midtown entertainment culture.

In Detroit, the sheer size of its 142 square miles coupled with the amount of vacancy and abandonment has made the challenge of providing basic human services difficult. Into this breach have stepped powerful neighborhood organizations and privately funded social service organizations, a large cadre of volunteers, and, in extreme cases, a form of "vigilantism" to help provide safe and secure neighborhoods. Occasionally this self-reliant culture can result in anarchy, no more obviously demonstrated than by the current practice of some citizens and law enforcement personnel alike of ignoring traffic signals.

The compassionate hard-working Detroit resident has to be seen in contrast to the drug and gang culture that receives a disproportionate amount of publicity. This, in turn, has to be seen

1 West Warren Road, Detroit. 2004

2 Empty sign at Schoolcraft Road and Standsbury Street, Detroit. 2004

3 Empty sign at Grand River Avenue and Robson Street, Detroit. 2004

1

CRUSADE
A&A
LIQUOR
2
3

chili's

against the background of race—the unspoken "elephant" that dominates everything in Detroit. The growing proportion of "minorities" in the city is directly proportional to the avoidance of the city by suburbanites. Joblessness, extreme poverty, "block busting," "redlining," and other ills of the shrinking city can be directly tied to racial bias. Likewise, enterprises such as the governance of the Detroit Institute of Arts or the control of the regional water system have an underlying racial foundation in that any proposal to remove control from the city to a larger regional or state entity is tainted with the message "African Americans cannot efficiently and profitably run a large enterprise or business." This antipathy between white suburb and black city is best illustrated by the fact that the city bus system does not connect seamlessly to the regional bus system. Racial tensions permeate all transactions.

My love for Detroit began with the hearty souls who occupy the city because they are reminiscent of the rural farming families among whom I spent my childhood. Their inventiveness, individualism, persistence, and ability to deal with enormous daily frustrations are a constant wonderment. The "frontier" mentality that dominates large areas of Detroit is illustrative of great opportunity. It is also a mentality that is less concerned with race than with individual fortitude. There are a host of creative urban experiments taking place throughout the city that illustrate this individualism. These include large-scale urban farming enterprises, guerilla gardening, ad hoc public transportation systems, green building experiments, "found object" constructions, food cooperatives, co-housing enclaves, and vigorous art and music installations and performances. The city is ripe with opportunities for cultural experimentation—with or without the approbation of government. It is not surprising that the residents who have stuck it out have been joined by those from around the world seeking a different way of living than that advertised daily in the mass media as the "American way of life."

1,2 Gratiot Avenue, Roseville, Metro Detroit. 2004

2

It was in this cultural cauldron that the International Center for Urban Ecology (iCUE) was formed. Initiated by Kyong Park, Andrew Zago and Stephen Vogel, iCUE, with Park as a driving force, has sought to examine the post-industrial city from a fresh perspective and articulate the ironies of Detroit's current condition. It is through these ironies that a non-traditional approach to the creation of a future post-industrial city might be discovered. This future city has not been previously visualized in traditional urban planning textbooks, which are typically based on the premise of growth and prosperity. What type of city might be premised on population shrinkage, collective individualism, economic classlessness, subsistence economics, and the arts? ICUE, by bringing international artists, scholars, and pragmatists into collaboration with Detroit's grassroots organizations and individuals, has generated a body of work that triggers the imagination and portends a "brave new world." It is through the vision and work of Park and others described in this book that we are offered a glimpse of this world.

Cities today are experiencing a crisis. For more than a century they have been used as the raw material with which to realize ideological agendas. They have been molded to represent a single social philosophy, to serve a single industry, or to perform a single dominant function. This overlay has suppressed their role as venues for social and political freedom and has collided with their intrinsically multifarious nature. Schisms have formed. In tandem with the existence of wealthy urban enclaves, older cities are marked by zones of large-scale disinvestment, calculated neglect, and abandonment.

In this process, creative professionals have complacently served the agents of urban crisis. They helped conceive and implement projects that destroyed vital cities. As a result of this malfeasance, art and architecture have forfeited their critical role in shaping cities and the public has largely forgotten the emancipating potential of urban space. Creative professionals must now forge a new role for themselves. By enmeshing art and architecture into the political and social life of cities, by creating works in concert with the imagination and aspirations of communities, and by working against the tidy logic of monolithic plans, they can promote an architecture of resistance.

An architecture of resistance works at the root of cities. It works with the varied and viable strands of existing communities. It views the city as an ecosystem rather than a machine; an orchestration of a fluid and organic infrastructure. In this view, new projects are seen as catalysts rather than as ends in themselves. Art and architecture function as conduits for public imagination, allowing a community to create its own social and public space. It promotes an urbanism that is liberating. It returns the maintenance and advancement of democracy to where it began: the city.

Detroit demonstrates the terminal stages of twentieth-century urbanism. Here, the city became a factory, its workers brought in and housed like parts for the automobiles they assembled. Then, like a factory, it became obsolete and was discarded in the perpetual and illusory search for unsullied land and an unsullied work force. While Detroit starkly prefigures other cities now enjoying the fruits of economic expansion, it also potentially holds the future hope of urbanism. Detroit, a city whose scale of urban abandonment is unparalleled, a city which serves as a poster child for the legacy of mass production, a city which perfected the oxymoron of unskilled labor, is a city in which an architecture of resistance can begin.

Terminal City

Andrew Zago

Architecture of Resistance

A workshop
Near eastside, Detroit (1999)

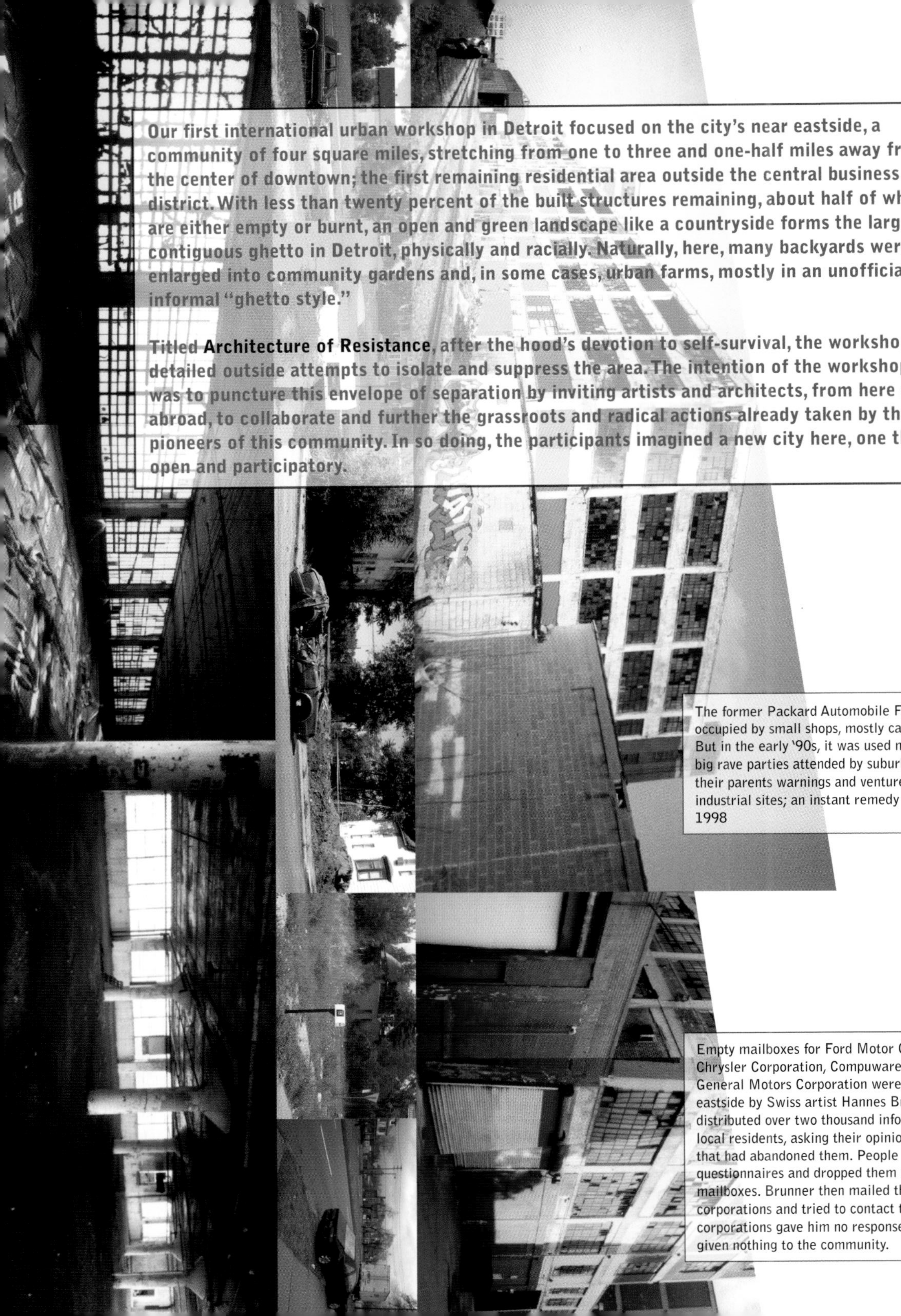

Our first international urban workshop in Detroit focused on the city's near eastside, a community of four square miles, stretching from one to three and one-half miles away from the center of downtown; the first remaining residential area outside the central business district. With less than twenty percent of the built structures remaining, about half of which are either empty or burnt, an open and green landscape like a countryside forms the largest contiguous ghetto in Detroit, physically and racially. Naturally, here, many backyards were enlarged into community gardens and, in some cases, urban farms, mostly in an unofficial and informal "ghetto style."

Titled **Architecture of Resistance**, after the hood's devotion to self-survival, the workshop detailed outside attempts to isolate and suppress the area. The intention of the workshop was to puncture this envelope of separation by inviting artists and architects, from here and abroad, to collaborate and further the grassroots and radical actions already taken by the pioneers of this community. In so doing, the participants imagined a new city here, one that is open and participatory.

The former Packard Automobile Factory is now partly occupied by small shops, mostly car-related businesses. But in the early '90s, it was used more infamously for big rave parties attended by suburban kids who defied their parents warnings and ventured into the city's wild industrial sites; an instant remedy to suburban monotony. 1998

Empty mailboxes for Ford Motor Company, Daimler/Chrysler Corporation, Compuware Corporation, and General Motors Corporation were installed in the near eastside by Swiss artist Hannes Brunner. He hand-distributed over two thousand informal questionnaires to local residents, asking their opinion of the corporations that had abandoned them. People responded to the questionnaires and dropped them in these corporate mailboxes. Brunner then mailed the replies to the corporations and tried to contact them, but the corporations gave him no response, just as they have given nothing to the community.

Mr. Franklin, a year-round bicycle rider, lives on Farnsworth near Chene Street. 1998

Stolen and stripped cars are often disposed here, along with abandoned "ghetto cruisers" — fifty to two hundred dollar cars that are dumped when they break. People simply buy another car with that money, which usually is cheaper than fixing the car. There is also "on order" stealing of cars, which is an ingenious example of the gray economy. A car is stolen according to the type, color, and specification desired by a potential buyer. It is stripped of major parts, to make it beyond repair. The people who stole it then notify the police, who usher in the insurance company, which inspects it and declares it to be "totaled." A towing truck is then summoned, and the same people who stole the car show up with the tow truck. They are paid and given a temporary registration of the car for towing it. The stripped parts are replaced, and the car is in running condition again, ready to be sold to the person who ordered it at the beginning of this game. The old car is officially dead, but reborn with a new legal registration. 1997-2002

VPRO, a Dutch television station, interviewing Lee Burns. A property owner in the near eastside of Detroit, he began large-scale gardening there, envisioning the self-generation of a new community under his concept called Lifeland. The Dutch documentary *Detroit Comeback City* also featured Derrick May, Juan Atkinson, Kevin Sanderson, Stephen Vogel, Kyong Park, and others. 1997

Canvas is used to catch rain that seeps through the roof and floors at the former Packard Automobile Plant. A once-mighty factory now bandages its wounds with mere cloth. 1998

Earth walls, more than twenty-five feet high and a half-mile long, were built to block streets and to separate the west side of the Jefferson Assembly Plant of Daimler/Chrysler from the surrounding neighborhood. Was the Chrysler Corporation trying to protect its valuable investment from the burning city, or was it afraid of future racial riots, and people stealing the new cars and machines? Much has changed since the days when the automobile industries built houses for their workers so they could live right next to the factory. 1998

A ten-foot concrete block wall divides the east side of the Jefferson Assembly Plant of Daimler/Chrysler from the surrounding neighborhood. But the five hundred feet of open fields between the wall and the plant look strangely like a demilitarized zone. 1998

S.P.O.R.E. (*Sustainable Projects Organized in Respect to the Environment*) was proposed by Mel Chin (Burnsville, North Carolina), who imagined that the infamy of Devil's Night fire-charred houses could be superseded by surreal and pragmatic economic interventions. In one plan, the roof of an empty house is dropped to just above the basement, its wooden framing members ground to sawdust creating nourishment for gourmet mushrooms, grown to be sold to fancy restaurants. In another, a house pivots to reveal a basement breeding worms to be marketed to sport fishing industries. Chin envisioned many surreal structures evolving from the stigmatized remains, and new economies nurtured by the urban ruins.

Marcos van Steekelenburg (the Netherlands) proposed that empty lots between houses be linked to make a very unusual golf course. Can a culture of prosperity and leisure be recontextualized within a community of poverty and survival?

An installation inside the iCUE studio by Clemens Austen (Kiel, Germany) resembles a spider web that seems as if it could easily cover the city. It also provokes a thought that the destruction, and even the reconstruction, of the city could spread in a similar manner.

Andre Vovk, from Michael Sorkin's studio (New York).

Slide projection by G. Todd Roberts and Kyong Park, assisted by Kiersten Armstrong. An image of a suburban mansion from Gross Pointe Shores, one of the wealthiest areas in the suburbs of Detroit, was projected on a burnt house at Mitchell and West Canfield Streets, an attempt to connect opposing locations to counter the fragmentation and segregation of Metro Detroit.

Mark Anderson (Seattle) and Andrew Zago (Detroit) proposed that an open pavilion be built using wood scavenged from abandoned houses. Surely this was inspired by the default environmental movement of the low economy. For instance, in the summer months, you can see many people pushing shopping carts full of scrap metal through the streets. This is when the price for scrap is highest, as the auto industry is producing the next year's models.

There were many houses that stood burnt for more than five years. Maybe there were simply too many burnt houses for the city to tear down immediately, but it is also possible that they were left there to create a visual scenario that would drive the price of real estate here down, so that the "conspirators" could buy the land for next to nothing. How else can the amount and nature of devastation in Detroit be explained? It just could not all be natural phenomena. 1997-2001

Site where a house was recently demolished, near the *Heidelberg Project*. Tracks from the bulldozer recall a farm field plowed to seed a new crop, making urban farming in the inner city seem logical. 1998

Craig Bachellier and Kyong Park imagined constructing architecture without program that could be fabricated like cars, perhaps at the old Packard plant nearby. The idea was to posit spaces in empty landscapes that could incubate future uses and events.

A roof being repaired to keep the house upright until a better time. Saint Aubin and Farnsworth Streets, 1997

In spite of empty and burnt houses all around, there are still many houses that are well kept, evidence of how tenacious and inspiring people can be.
Many houses are repaired with a mosaic of materials from demolished houses.

Architecture workshops for kids in the community, coordinated by Dada Flounary.

It was common to have a house fire everyday, especially in the summer of 2001. Many speculated that the projected redevelopment of the waterfront directly to the south was the reason. It felt like there was a rush to burn down the near eastside sooner than later. This area, the first adjacent residential sector to downtown, as well as to Lafayette Park and other urban renewal projects, is ideal for new residential developments. 1999

There are many melted and blackened walls in Detroit. Because houses were built so close together, one burning house will melt or burn houses on both sides. People often have to save their houses from burning with a garden hose, since the timely arrival of the fire department or police is not certain. Often both departments let buildings burn to the ground so they don't have to keep coming back to fight drugs or other troubles. 1999

Isabel Becker (Kiel, Germany) translated a series of drawings of houses into clay. She put these clay objects into garbage cans, and placed the cans inside empty houses that would most likely be burned, turning the houses into kilns and the clay into ceramics. Unfortunately or not, her project was never realized. One day the police came to the world headquarters of iCUE, asking why we had put garbage cans into empty houses. They thought the cans might contain dead babies or combustible materials. We explained that it was simply an art project. They replied "Oh," and left.

Theodore Street is where Paul Weertz began his urban farming. Shaded area shows where houses used to stand.

Adamah project meeting, with Grace Lee Boggs and Jim Embry (second from the right), respectively the founder and director of the Boggs Center. 2001

Property lines are invisible and unenforced. *De facto* ownership develops, and undeclared spaces are used for barbecues, weekend family gatherings, gardening, or parking cars. Often the added space is claimed by cutting its grass. The lawnmower becomes a property maker. 1999

In the spring, tall grass is everywhere, before the city gets a chance to cut it. The Farm-a-Lot program, which offered expertise and equipment to encourage citizens to grow food on empty lots, was begun by the city in 1974 in part to eliminate tall-grassed places that could conceal criminal activities. 1999

You will often see a well-kept house alone in a vast open landscape, recalling the early pioneering days of America. Adjacent lots can often be bought cheaply at state and city auctions of real estate, and priority has been given to sell the empty lots to adjacent homeowners. Side yards are becoming as common as back yards, 1997

The battle between paved and green surface is constant and everywhere. Surface parking lots, sidewalks, and roads are being attacked by nature, returning the city to its primordial state.

Paul Weertz, a legendary urban pioneer, farms about ten acres of land in the near eastside where a middle school once stood (corner of Canfield and Mount Elliot Streets). He also farms the land at Warren and Mitchell Streets where Northeast High School once was, and at Moran and Theodore Streets, where his residence and iCUE are located. Alfalfa is his favorite crop, as it nourishes the soil while extracting toxicity. Farming on public land is justified by the notion of ownership based on productive use, much like Native American belief.

But Weertz's greatest accomplishment may be at the Catherine Ferguson Academy. As its science teacher, he helps teenage mothers learn about caring for their kids through the lessons of growing food from the land. 1998

Paul Weertz demonstrates his new harvesting machine to fellow urban farmer Lee Burns. 1998

Inside John's Blues Club, an underground, or "over the grass" Sunday music dig. Friends are invited to this "blind pig" to enjoy a communal affair. This open theater is hidden inside a wall made of recycled carpets, stripped from empty houses. 1997

Feeling more confident, John has now moved the open theater outside of the carpet walls, creating a semi-permanent stage facing the street. Abandoned chairs, sofas, and benches are set up on the facing yard, inviting more people through visibility.

Beginning in 1986, artist Tyree Guyton used found objects and brightly colored polka dots to transform Heidelberg Street, where his family lives, into an urban oasis of hope and participation. The second most visited place in Detroit, the *Heidelberg Project* is a place where people can experience "creative and adaptive reuse of urban decay." Yet, controversy has always followed Guyton, as the city has twice demolished the project (1991 and 1999), even after bestowing upon him the "Spirit of Detroit Award" in 1989. But, in the true spirit of many native sons of this under-appreciated city, he fights back, now polka dotting abandoned buildings and houses all over Detroit, challenging the city to renovate or demolish them. 1997

Is the informal city—as the barrios in Caracas are technically called—a parasite that lives off the formal city? Do street sellers live off the service economy? Would the informal city, and the informal economy it entails, collapse with the demise of the formal city, as parasites do when a host dies?

I don't think so. In my view, informal strategies are systems that parallel formal ones. Although perceived by the modern city as disorganized, ephemeral, perhaps even catastrophic strategies, they operate successfully using their own sets of rules. What such informal strategies have in common is the fact that they prosper within unbalanced urban realities, such as fast-growing or fast-shrinking cities. In Caracas, two such strategies have developed that complement each other: the informal city and the informal economy.

The Informal City

In the '60s and '70s, Caracas was one of the world's fastest growing cities thanks to the accelerated development of the oil industry there. The rapid expansion of the formal city caused an influx of supporting service economies. Construction workers migrated from the rural inland, built the formal city and, at the same time, built the informal city for themselves. Caracas today is a sharply divided city; it is, in fact, an entity made up of two cities forced to coexist in close proximity. The informal city was not planned. It was initiated by individuals who settled on public land without obtaining permits. The informal trading of informal property functions well here. The informal city is a self-initiated and self-upgrading structure.

Today, Caracas is a city in the midst of social and economic crisis. Mismanagement of the largest state enterprise, the oil industry, has destabilized the formal city and caused the economy to shrink. The informal economy, which is how barrio residents make their living, remains aggressively vital.

The social state never really materialized in Caracas and, for the half of the city's population that lives in the barrios, has been virtually nonexistent. Only recently have land titles been distributed to barrio residents in an effort to integrate the illegal population. Large-scale systems, such as the city's energy and utility infrastructures, have completely failed the barrios. Barrio residents

Informal City and Informal Economy

Marjetica Potrč

usually steal electricity by tapping into the power grid, and the city provides water to barrios only irregularly—twice per week for a few hours. Residents are forced to rely on their own ingenuity. Private and public are balanced in creative ways. There is, for instance, no public space *per se* in the barrios; all public space is privately negotiated. Representational architecture does not exist. The barrios accommodate libraries, schools, and hospitals, but such buildings look like any other barrio structure, and do not present a formal face. Here is another example: if a family wants to add a new floor to their house, they negotiate the upgrading with their neighbors and the community. Consensus is reached through spoken, not written agreements, a strategy considered primitive in the formal city.

The Informal Economy

Public space in the formal city is occupied—some would say invaded—by street sellers, who set up their stands on streets and walkways daily, thus making their temporary status permanent and transforming public spaces into open-air informal markets. Some vendors do not even have street stands; they sell their goods on the highways. They take advantage of the city's frequent traffic jams, walking onto the highways and then off again, depending on whether the cars are moving fast or slow. I heard that one of the department stores hires street sellers to hawk its goods on the highways. In this way, the highly structured formal economy tips its hat to the informal economy, conceding that it is a model that functions well.

On the face of it, Caracas is a city in permanent crisis, but it presents us with a reality check—a case study, so to speak—that is generally applicable to the contemporary postmodern urban condition, where private space is valued more than public space; where temporary but durable values are emerging with unprecedented vigor; where privacy and security are enhanced; where mutually alien communities coexist in close proximity and constantly have to adjust to one other; where a seemingly regressive return to archetypal models such as gated communities and shantytowns is common; where self-sustainability is part of the working model, whether this means self-reliance regarding basic energy and communication infrastructures, the construction of individual homes, or the informal trading of goods.

The informal city and the informal economy used to be considered alien urban forms, and were sometimes compared to invasions of the rural into the urban. What constitutes the urban fabric today? Can one mention the urban and the rural in one and the same breath? Can partial and self-sustainable solutions be successful? Can an individual make a significant contribution to complex dynamic systems? Two things come to mind. First, the World Bank has been recommending small-scale urban agriculture for fast-growing cities like Cairo. Imagine family vegetable gardens appearing on the roofs of a city. Second, GNU/Linux, a successful computer operating system, is constantly being improved by volunteer programmers. It seems that individuals can, indeed, balance the equilibrium between the self and the other with good results.

1,2 Marjetica Potrč, *Dry Toilet*, building materials and sanitation infrastructure, Caracas (photo: Andre Cypriano © 2003)

1

2

The report *Skopje Resurgent* [1] published by the United Nations in 1970 documents the reconstruction of Skopje after a major earthquake in 1963. Following a UN resolution, an international group of architects, city planners, and experts from other disciplines were mobilized to work out a concept for the rebuilding of the city. Prefabricated homes and apartments, schools, lecture rooms, and other facilities were donated to Skopje by more than sixty countries.

The UN resolution became a temporary laboratory of experts from various disciplines, nationalities, and ideological perspectives to formulate a "Master Plan" for the reconstruction. The plan included a number of innovative experimental technical and scientific initiatives that were quickly implemented. The winning design for the UN competition for the reconstruction of the city was by the Japanese architect and urban planner Kenzo Tange. An adaptation of his radical plan for a new city in the Tokyo Bay in 1960, the Skopje scheme appears in Tange's monographs only in model form.

Despite the inevitable revisions and miscalculations (for example, an over-scale rail station intended for high-speed transport between Athens and Paris and unexpected wind turbulence between the buildings that had been intended to create the "City Wall"), Tange's plan remains intact and constitutes the structure for Skopje today. Taking into consideration decades of political transformation and economic complications, the improvised urban structure of the suburbs of Skopje, much of which initially intended to function on a temporary basis, has become permanent with constant adaptations. As the street names attest (many named after the capital cities contributing to the reconstruction effort), the combined efforts of informal and collaborative professional planning may function as an interesting model for future consideration.

Excerpts from the UN's *Skopje Resurgent* document:

. . . this display of solidarity expressed, in its own way, the strivings towards new, more humane relations in the world, of relations wherein the welfare of each and every nation would be in the interest of the world community as a whole. Eventually more than sixty countries furnished technical assistance of one kind or another, and twenty-five of them participated directly in the physical re-planning and reconstruction of the city.

Solidarity Architecture and Kenzo Tange's Urban Planning of Skopje

Sean Snyder

1 *Skopje Resurgent, The Story of a United Nations Special Fund Town Planning Project* (United Nations: New York, 1970).

. . . any planning that was done for Skopje had to take account of the fact that the earthquake had created a revolutionary situation—not in the literary-cliché sense, but in the precise Marxist meaning of the term. It had given rise to needs that transcended the competence of established procedures. To meet them, standing orders had to be suspended; decision-making machinery improvised ad hoc, and contractual obligations taken on trust.

. . . "instant planning" exercises both informed and were informed by the progress of the work normally involved in the preparation of a master plan, making it impossible for the section responsible to adopt too academic or theoretical an approach to its main task. In the case of the social survey, the consequent involvement of sociologists in the planners' job, and vice versa, was a new experience for both, with no established principles to guide them.

A corps of eighty-five university students, with no previous experience of conducting interviews, had to be recruited, put through a thirty-hour course of training and tested. . . . The Social Survey Section was therefore obliged to concentrate in the first instance on those matters which had the greatest relevance to basic planning decisions, such as immigrants' motives for coming to Skopje, suburban families' shopping habits and social activities outside the home.

The questioning of families and institutions on a wide range of matters of fact and of opinion was supplemented by observations of social behavior and a close study of the processes of local self-government.

Schoolchildren in Skopje were told, as usual, to write an essay on "A major event in the life of my town." Four out of five chose as their subject the new Master Plan.

It was an experience shared by many professional specialists from all over the world, and through them its implications will doubtless be distilled, digested and absorbed into the body of technical and organizational expertise that informs the practice of town planning and related disciplines.

1,2 Kenzo Tange's planning model of Skopje, 1963-1971 (film still courtesy: The Cinematheque of Macedonia Archive, Skopje)

3 *Skopje*, 1963-1971 (film still courtesy: The Cinematheque of Macedonia architve, Skopje)

Although they are not always distinctive, formal and informal systems simultaneously exist in every society. A formal system cannot function without its informal counterpart, and *vice versa;* they supplement and react to one another. In an urban context, this proposition implies a new kind of thinking about an architect's impact on the evolution of the city. It suggests that directed assimilation of informal activities (chaos) can become a tool for achieving more formality (order). Therefore, urban planning can be seen as a "rhizomatic" interweaving of actions and programs that come from both the formal and the informal systems. As a result of such integration, a new and unpredictable process of urban communication emerges—the process I am terming urban navigation. The role of the architect is consequently redefined as well: he/she is a sensor, a provoker, and a guide through urban processes which do not result in a final order, but are left open-ended. Architectural intervention thus accompanies and inspires the ever-evolving process of sustainable urban development.

In economically less developed countries, informal systems can play a significant role because they can adapt themselves more flexibly to economic and political fluctuations. For instance, in crisis situations such as those witnessed in post-war Bosnia and Herzegovina, informal markets were for years the only functioning engines of the economy. The famous Arizona Market, one of the largest black markets in the Balkans, emerged as a reaction to the political and economic crisis after the war. Providing work for over 30,000 people in over 2,200 businesses,[1] the Arizona Market presents a unique opportunity to observe the birth of a self-planned city. Since the market came into being when a regulated state system did not exist, its creators were able to generate their own informal system. In this case, self-organization has been both a political and an economic success in the area, much more so than the official government. One of the most economically developed parts of Bosnia, the Arizona Market brought warring people together, becoming the first point of reconciliation in this war-torn country.

However, the market has now reached a critical size and its emerging communal problems can no longer be solved through individual action. Now is indeed the moment for the informal to be formalized. The market has already been self-regulating in terms of designating parking areas, developing traffic circulation systems, and assigning house numbers. Yet, many of its other problematic aspects, such as organized crime, disease epidemics, and fire risks are making the

Urban Navigation

Azra Aksamija

Arizona Market. Arizona Road, in northern Bosnia and Herzegovina (photo: Azra Aksamija © 2001)

1 Status of the Market in 2000. Estimation according to *Analysis of the Activities of the Arizona Market since its Establishment until June 2000* by the Government of Brcko Distrikt, Bosnia and Herzegovina, Department for Urbanism, Ownership Structures and Economic Development.

TAXI
843-M-068

inclusion of a formal system an urgent necessity. These pressing issues, as well as the regional interest in the market's economic success, have finally brought the district government to act. Unfortunately and not surprisingly, the government has responded by developing a master plan that proposes to turn the market into a shopping mall, eliminating all self-planned forms and imposing a higher order of urban development. The proposed shopping mall would make the market disappear, destroying the sustenance and the social network of people who created it. Institutionally supported conventional planning methods often tend to fight against informal elements, because these elements are spontaneous, flexible, and therefore completely unpredictable. The notion of control is the main drive behind urban projects developed in a formal (institutional) system and pursued through diverse master-plan urban strategies. Since the word "strategy" is a war term, the notion of "urban strategy" implies confrontational thinking. After all, urban planning is an expression of power and often a tool of oppression. The term "master plan" also indicates relations of power—who is the master? For whom is it planned? In cases of absolute dominance of the formal system, the results range from over-regulation to urban degeneration, which includes phenomena such as urban decay and shrinking. In cities such as Liverpool, England, for example, many projects developed through master planning did not succeed in revitalizing a city that suffered from urban degeneration. Indeed, large development projects can function only when their ultimate goal for order is achieved. But what are the larger implications if those goals are not reached? When residents themselves fail to provide initiative and are resigned to waiting for action and money from above, it is imperative to recognize that urban planning can no longer be an input-consumption system, but only a productive interaction of all parties involved. Urban navigation thus calls for a balance between formal and informal urbanism.

In economically more developed societies dominated by institutional regulation, the informal component is much smaller than the formal one, and is often relegated to "harmless" activities such as flea markets. How can more chaos be accepted in regulated surroundings? How can the informal condition be planned at all? While promoting a self-sustainable urban development, urban navigation seeks to find plausible solutions for provoking, learning, involving, and tracking a self-organized bottom-up methodology.

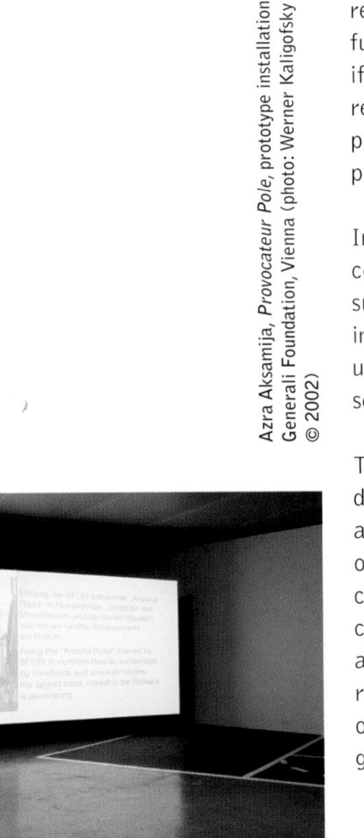

Azra Aksamija, *Provocateur Pole*, prototype installation. Generali Foundation, Vienna (photo: Werner Kaligofsky © 2002)

To rethink urban planning is to look at its problems with different eyes, to deal with them with different parameters, and to apply different concepts. Henri Lefebvre describes our "blindness" as result of seeing "with eyes, with concepts, that were shaped by the practices and theories of industrialization."[2] Urban navigation is a method of informal provocation. It uses existing conditions to create new ones which the next generation has to come to terms with—this cycle continuously reshapes urban conditions and communication processes through discovery, annexation, occupation, taking, stealing, and negotiation. The end goal of such development remains uncertain, as the aim is no longer to develop a new final order. The inclusion of self-organization indicates the acceptance of chaos and new urban solutions, allowing for potential growth, as well as failure.

2 Henri Lefebvre, *The Urban Revolution*, trans. Robert Bononno (Minneapolis and London: University of Minnesota Press, 2003), 29.

0 (miles from center)

General Motors World Headquarters
(The Renaissance Center)
Detroit

Detroit: Making It Better for You (A Fiction)

Two-channel video, 09.28 minutes
Metro Detroit (2000)

0,5

0,2

Detroit Edison Headquarters
Detroit

The Guardian Building
Detroit

Detroit: Making It Better for You is a gritty tapestry of images on the destruction of Detroit, a city struggling to sustain its communities in the face of global economic greed. The video's "drive-by-shooting" style is emblematic of the mythology of Detroit as both the "Motor City" and the "Murder City." It offers street-level views of the urban clashes between inner-city realities and suburban myths.

45% **The percentage of decline in the number of manufacturing, wholesale and retail establishments in Detroit [1972-1991]**

339 **The number of Ford Motor Company's full-time employees in Detroit**

We, the corporations, are ready to build a new city here in Detroit. Our plan, which began fifty years ago, is now almost complete. The entire city will soon be under our control. The government, desperate for jobs and money, is willing to give us big tax breaks and build roads and parks for us. We have successfully raised taxes, increased living costs, and used eminent domain and other legal and illegal means to force the residents to sell out and get out. The new city will be built according to our design and concept. We took land away from the natives, and now we are taking it from the disenfranchised and uneducated black underclass that currently lives in the slum that is Detroit. We have a clean slate with which to start fresh.

Here is how our plan has worked:

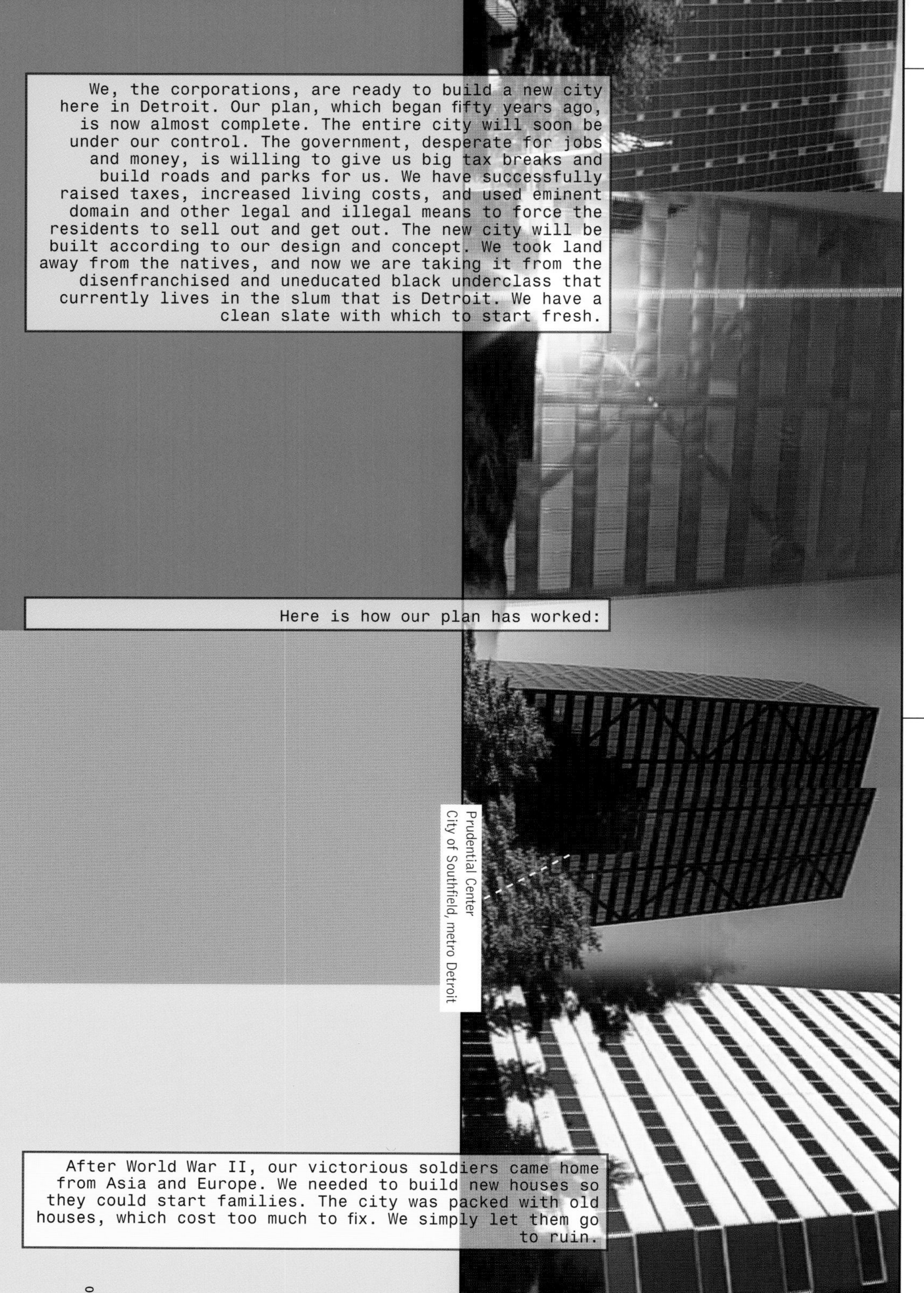

Prudential Center
City of Southfield, metro Detroit

After World War II, our victorious soldiers came home from Asia and Europe. We needed to build new houses so they could start families. The city was packed with old houses, which cost too much to fix. We simply let them go to ruin.

24,5

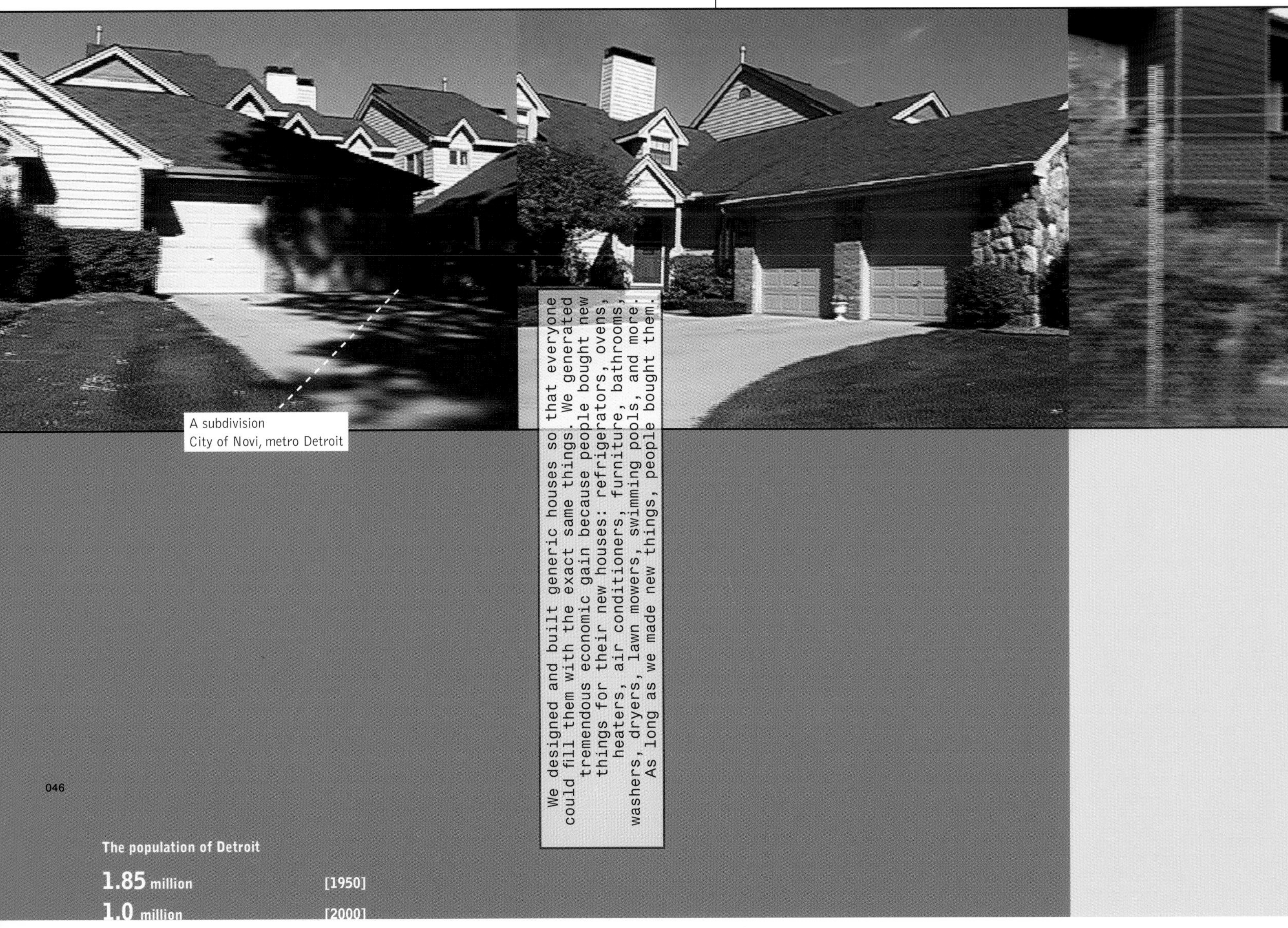

A subdivision
City of Novi, metro Detroit

We designed and built generic houses so that everyone could fill them with the exact same things. We generated tremendous economic gain because people bought new things for their new houses: refrigerators, ovens, heaters, air conditioners, furniture, bathrooms, washers, dryers, lawn mowers, swimming pools, and more. As long as we made new things, people bought them.

The population of Detroit

1.85 million [1950]

1.0 million [2000]

6,8

24,5

6,8

We then built bigger, more expensive houses, farther and farther away from the city. People bought the newer houses and filled them again, with our newer products. We successfully made consumerism a mass addiction.

Abandoned housing project, Detroit

But we needed to do more; we needed to keep the newly created, massive white middle class in constant motion to increase our profits exponentially. So we realized that our plan would require nothing less than the total destruction of the city of Detroit.

The population of Southeastern Michigan, outside of Detroit

1.5 million [1950]

4 million [2000]

24,5

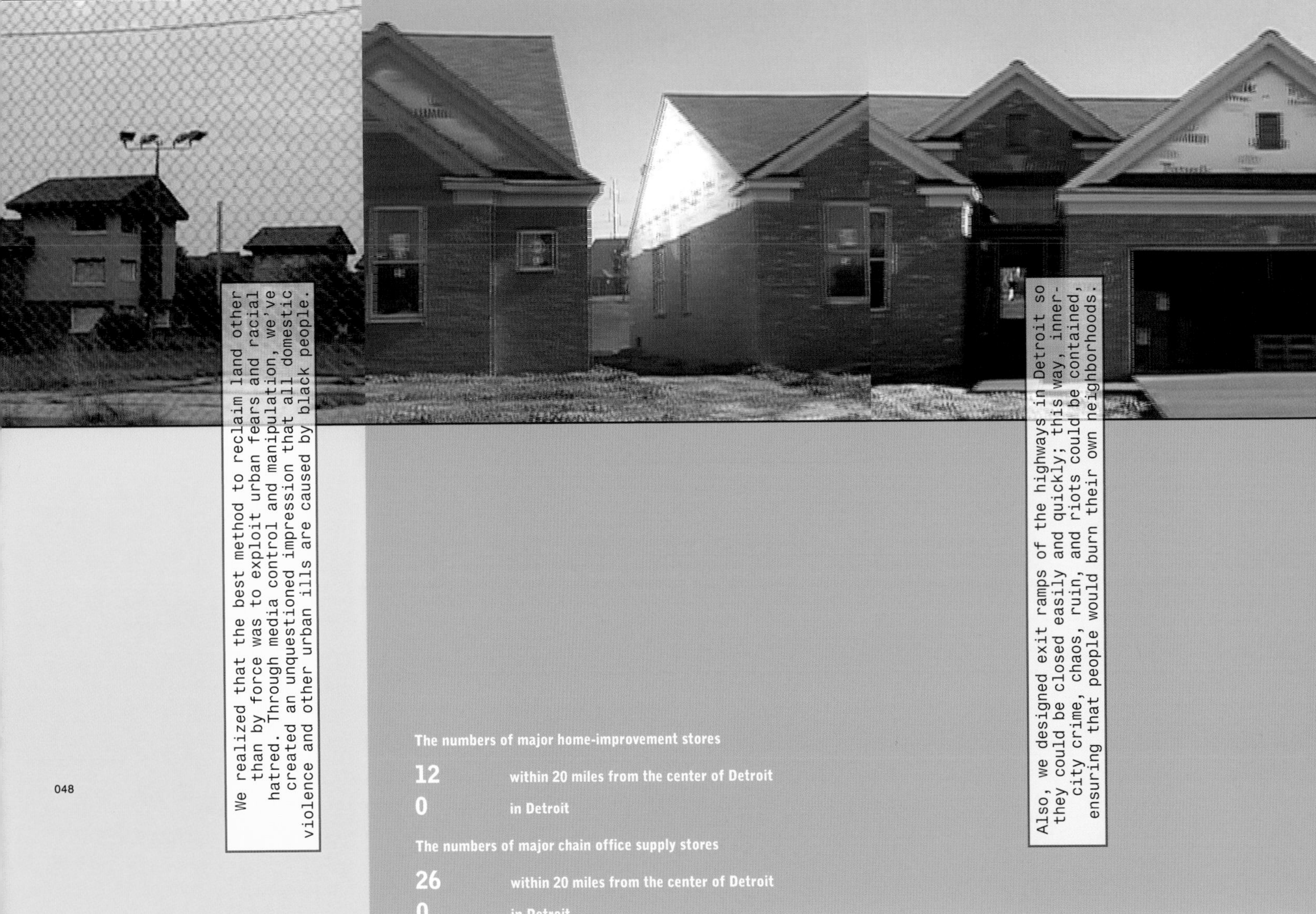

We realized that the best method to reclaim land other than by force was to exploit urban fears and racial hatred. Through media control and manipulation, we've created an unquestioned impression that all domestic violence and other urban ills are caused by black people.

Also, we designed exit ramps of the highways in Detroit so they could be closed easily and quickly; this way, inner-city crime, chaos, ruin, and riots could be contained, ensuring that people would burn their own neighborhoods.

The numbers of major home-improvement stores

12	**within 20 miles from the center of Detroit**
0	**in Detroit**

The numbers of major chain office supply stores

26	**within 20 miles from the center of Detroit**
0	**in Detroit**

6

5

Then we moved all our big factories out of Detroit, and then all other businesses, stores, and even gas stations followed us. But we let the liquor stores stay, to successfully pollute the mind and soul of city people. We've made damn sure that it's easier to get guns, drugs, and sex in Detroit than voter registration. We let the people there just keep on killing each other. We made Detroit so violent that people continue to flee from it, just like from a war zone. With their lives in danger, city residents sell their properties fast and low.

Lincoln Street
City of Highland Park,
metro Detroit

This set the stage for the disinvestment and total abandonment of the inner city. It became impossible to build new houses and buildings there because nobody would loan the money. All new houses and buildings were built exclusively in the suburbs.

The numbers of multiplex cinemas

22	**within 20 miles from the center of Detroit**
0	**in Detroit**

The numbers of super bookstores

14	**within 25 miles from the center of Detroit**
0	**in Detroit**

Victoria Park development, Detroit

We've also undermined Detroit's education system by pulling out funds and corrupting school officials. We've crowded the classes, paid less to teachers, and supplied no new books nor built new libraries. Our goal has been to make the entire population of Detroit illiterate and unqualified for any professional work.

The amount of money and equipment donated to the Public Schools [1999/2000 school year]

$519,000	Detroit
$18,000,000	Chicago

The amount of donations contributed to the Detroit Public Schools [between 1995/96FY and 1999/2000FY]

$293,426	by Daimler/Chrysler AG
$15,000	by Ford Motor Company
$2,050	by General Motors Corporation

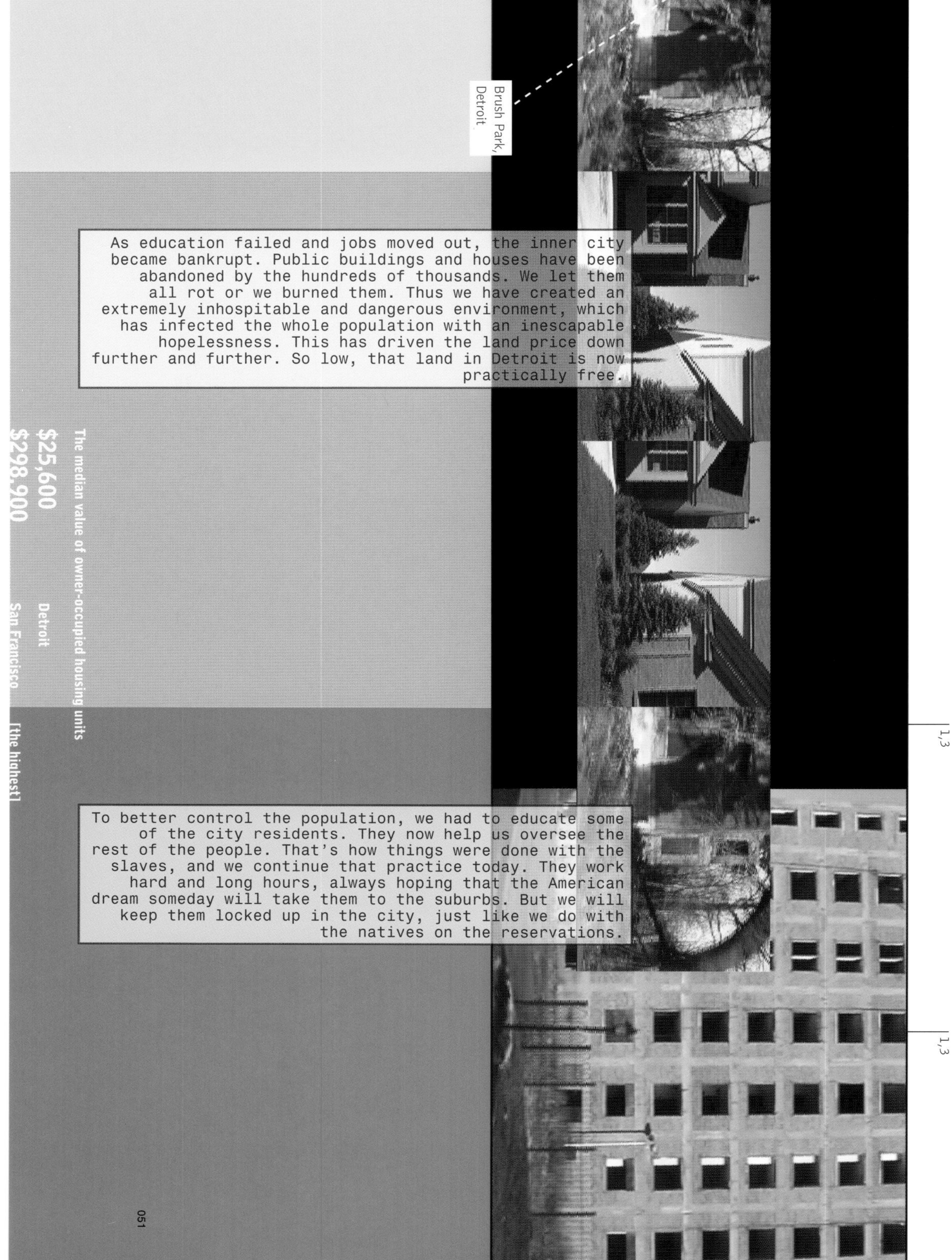

Brush Park, Detroit

As education failed and jobs moved out, the inner city became bankrupt. Public buildings and houses have been abandoned by the hundreds of thousands. We let them all rot or we burned them. Thus we have created an extremely inhospitable and dangerous environment, which has infected the whole population with an inescapable hopelessness. This has driven the land price down further and further. So low, that land in Detroit is now practically free.

To better control the population, we had to educate some of the city residents. They now help us oversee the rest of the people. That's how things were done with the slaves, and we continue that practice today. They work hard and long hours, always hoping that the American dream someday will take them to the suburbs. But we will keep them locked up in the city, just like we do with the natives on the reservations.

1,3

1,3

The median value of owner-occupied housing units

$25,600	**Detroit**	
$298,900	**San Francisco**	**[the highest]**

2,8 3,5 1,7

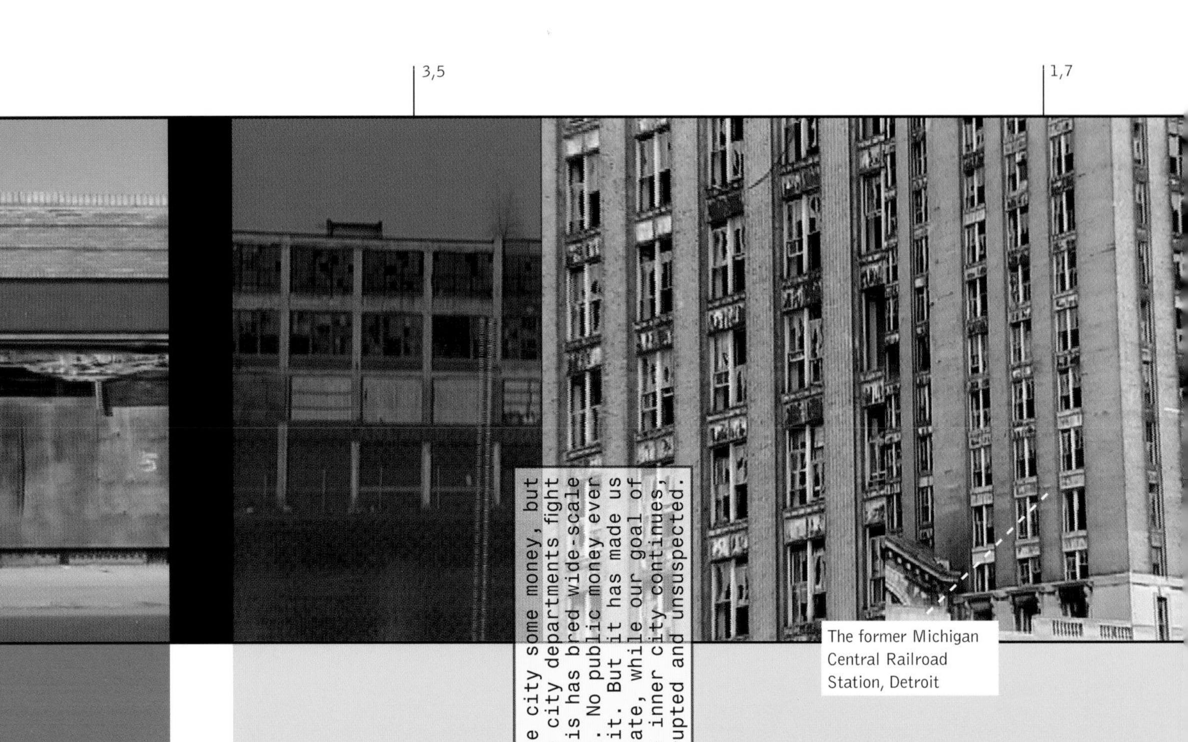

Chene Street, Detroit

Occasionally, we've given the city some money, but never quite enough. All the city departments fight among themselves for it, and this has bred wide-scale corruption and graft in Detroit. No public money ever gets to the people that need it. But it has made us look generous and compassionate, while our goal of the complete destruction of the inner city continues, uninterrupted and unsuspected.

The former Michigan Central Railroad Station, Detroit

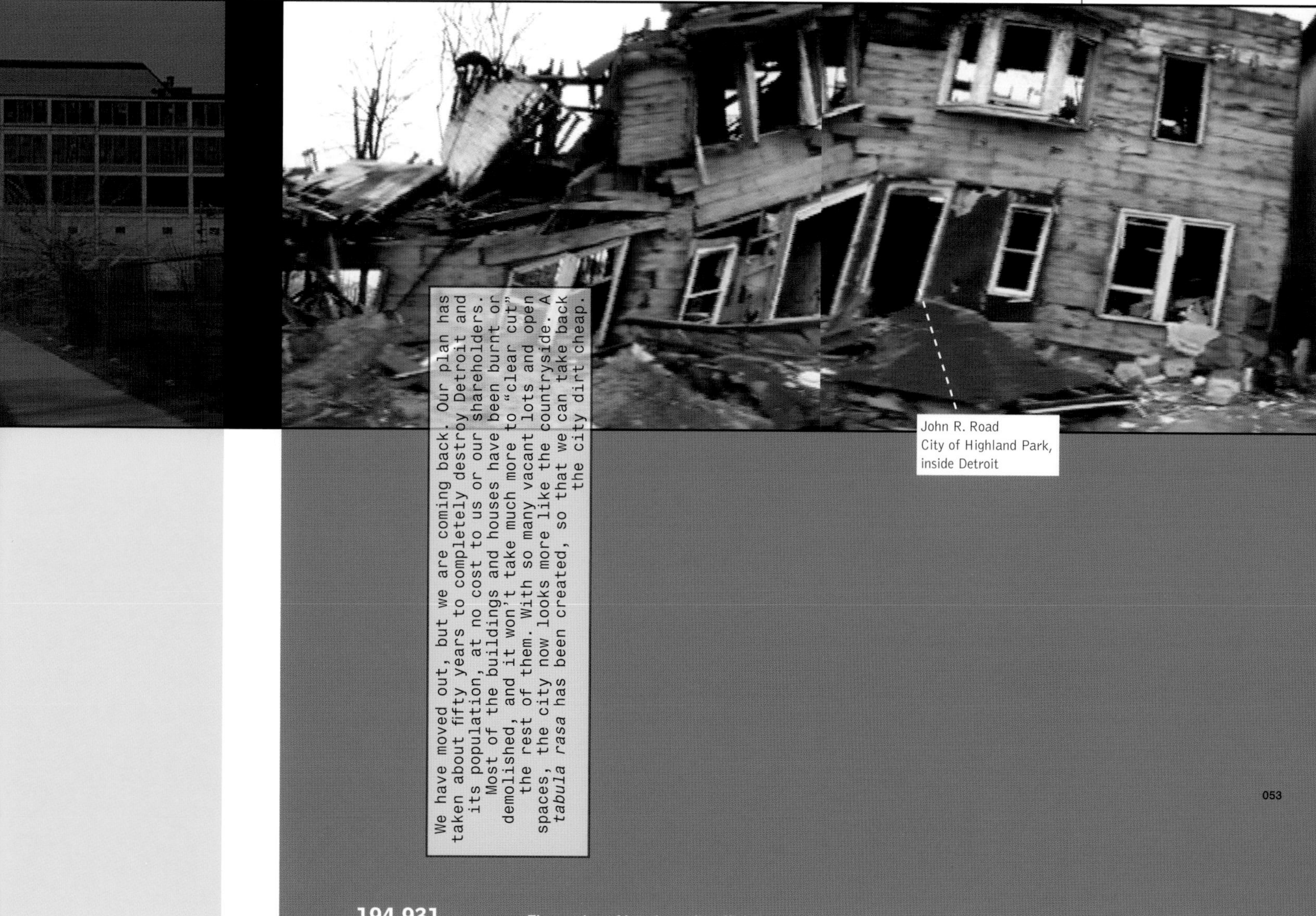

We have moved out, but we are coming back. Our plan has taken about fifty years to completely destroy Detroit and its population, at no cost to us or our shareholders.

Most of the buildings and houses have been burnt or demolished, and it won't take much more to "clear cut" the rest of them. With so many vacant lots and open spaces, the city now looks more like the countryside. A *tabula rasa* has been created, so that we can take back the city dirt cheap.

John R. Road
City of Highland Park,
inside Detroit

194,931 **The number of housing units officially demolished in Detroit** **[1960-2000]**

2,8

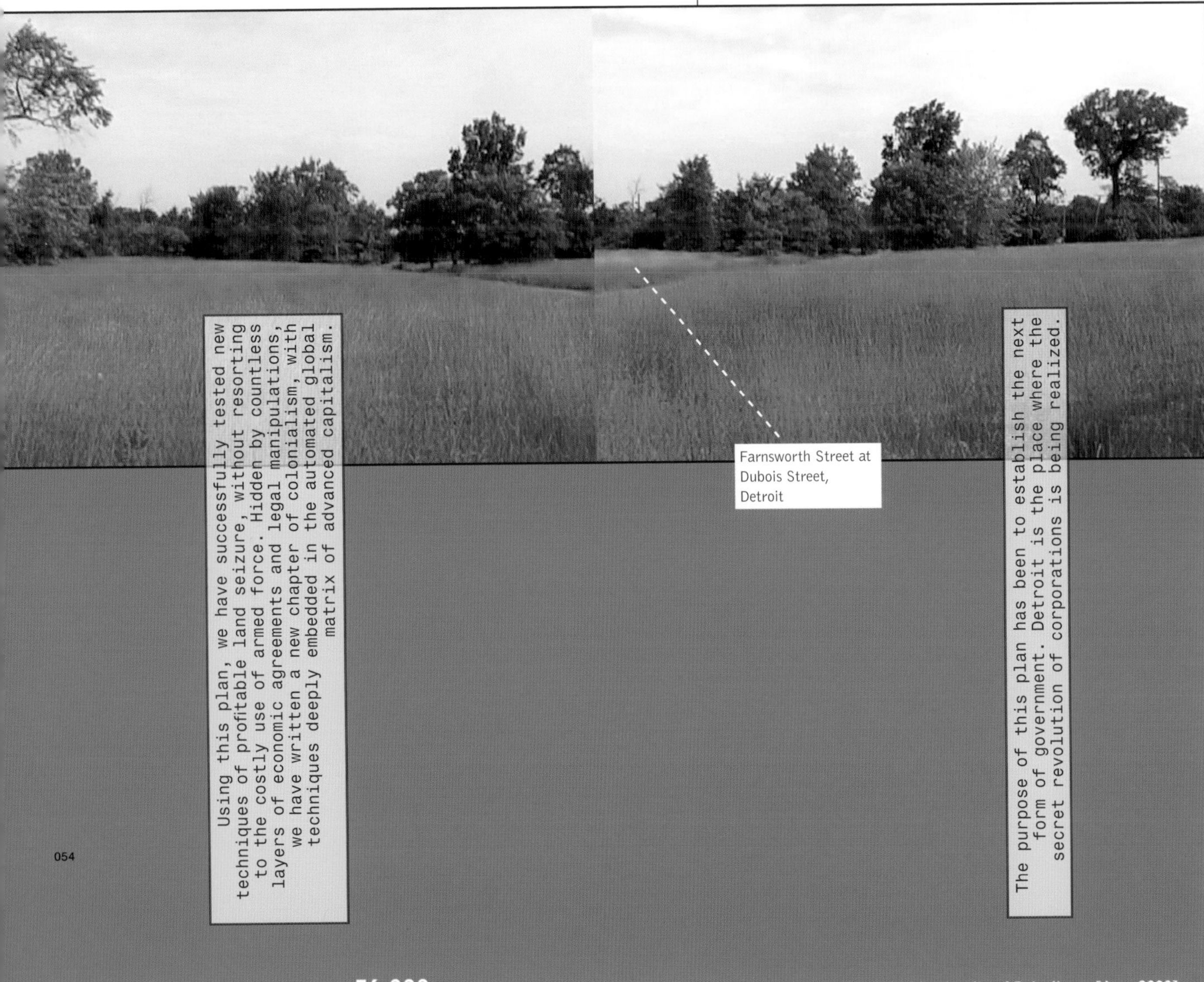

Farnsworth Street at Dubois Street, Detroit

Using this plan, we have successfully tested new techniques of profitable land seizure, without resorting to the costly use of armed force. Hidden by countless layers of economic agreements and legal manipulations, we have written a new chapter of colonialism, with techniques deeply embedded in the automated global matrix of advanced capitalism.

The purpose of this plan has been to establish the next form of government. Detroit is the place where the secret revolution of corporations is being realized.

56,000 The number of abandoned houses and vacant lots owned by the city of Detroit [June 2000]

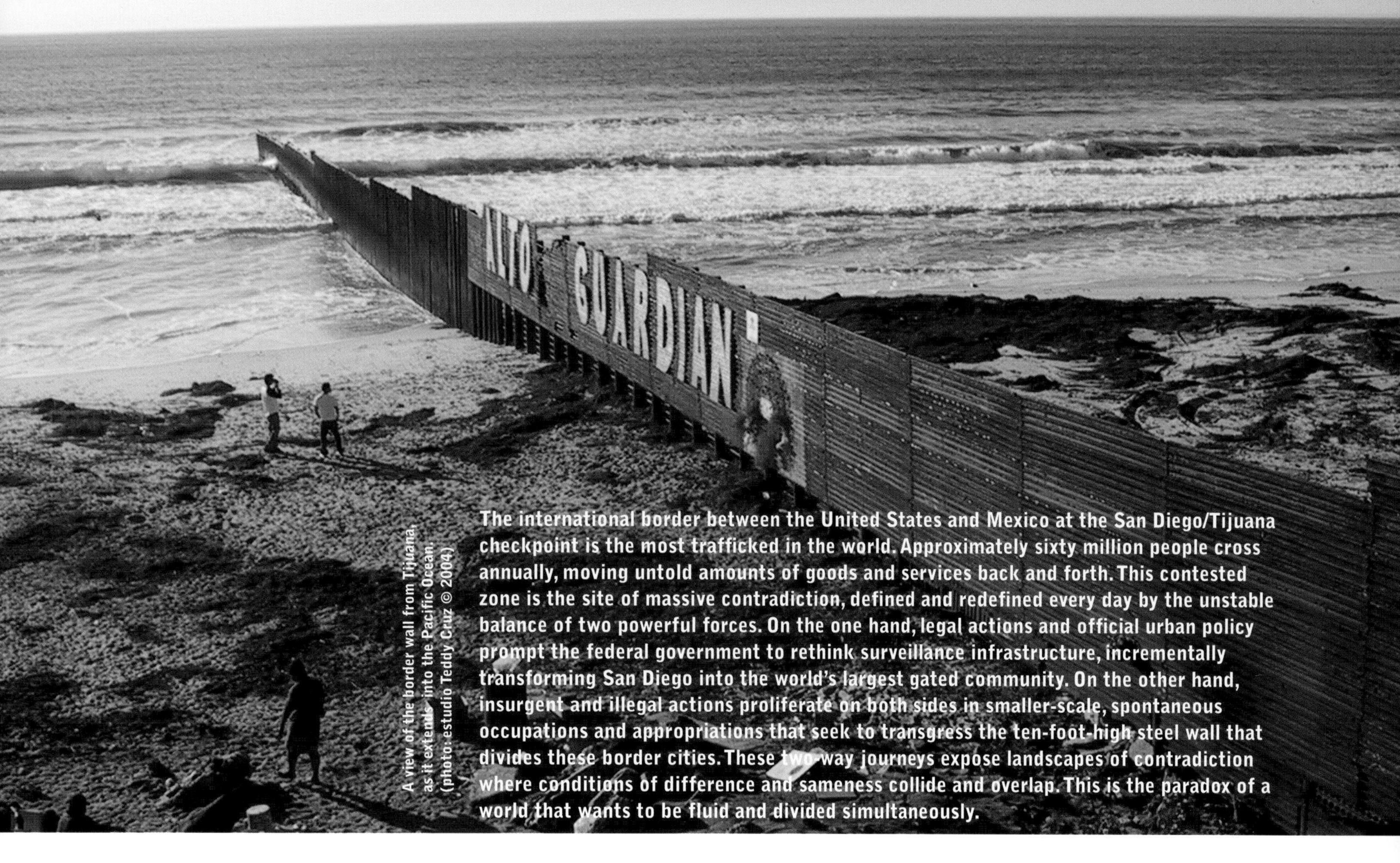

A view of the border wall from Tijuana, as it extends into the Pacific Ocean. (photo: estudio Teddy Cruz © 2004)

The international border between the United States and Mexico at the San Diego/Tijuana checkpoint is the most trafficked in the world. Approximately sixty million people cross annually, moving untold amounts of goods and services back and forth. This contested zone is the site of massive contradiction, defined and redefined every day by the unstable balance of two powerful forces. On the one hand, legal actions and official urban policy prompt the federal government to rethink surveillance infrastructure, incrementally transforming San Diego into the world's largest gated community. On the other hand, insurgent and illegal actions proliferate on both sides in smaller-scale, spontaneous occupations and appropriations that seek to transgress the ten-foot-high steel wall that divides these border cities. These two-way journeys expose landscapes of contradiction where conditions of difference and sameness collide and overlap. This is the paradox of a world that wants to be fluid and divided simultaneously.

Border Postcards: Chronicles from the Edge

Teddy Cruz

North to South: Disposable Housing

A Tijuana speculator travels to San Diego to buy up little bungalows that have been slated for demolition to make space for new condominium projects. The little houses are loaded onto trailers and prepared to travel to Tijuana, where they will have to clear customs before making their journey south. For days, one can see the houses, just like cars and pedestrians, waiting in line to cross the border. Finally the houses enter Tijuana and are mounted on one-story metal frames that leave an empty space at the street level to accommodate future uses. One city profits from the material that the other one wastes. Tijuana recycles the leftover buildings of San Diego, recombining them in fresh scenarios, creating countless new opportunities.

South to North: Flexible Urbanism

Increasing waves of immigration from Latin America have had a major impact on the urbanism of American cities. The immigrants bring with them their socio-cultural attitudes and sensibilities regarding the use of domestic and public space as well as the natural landscape. In their neighborhoods, multi-generational households of extended families shape their own programs of use, taking charge of their own mini economies in order to maintain a standard for the household. They generate illegal, non-conforming uses and high densities that reshape the fabric of the residential neighborhoods where they settle. Alleys, setbacks, driveways, and other wasted infrastructures and leftover spaces are appropriated and utilized, suggesting an urban operative process made of hybrid and flexible landscapes that transcend fixed architectural notions of style and typology.

In a "zero-setback" condition, San Diego retreats from the border, generating a hostile no-man's land between. On one side is a landscape of desire and necessity, but on the other is a landscape of fear and surveillance. (photos: estudio Teddy Cruz © 2004)

1

S

On a gray November evening it was all over; a few sharp wounds of open space were cut into the city fabric and the open landscape. In December I came to see for the first time what was left of the Iron Curtain. Only when lying like a corpse, its powerful and terrifying life discharged through a few small pokes along its many thousands of kilometers, was it possible to get near it, even to touch it.

H

The first time I went to see it—it was a giant trench cut through fields and olive orchards. Nothing seemed different from across its sides—the hills, orchards, and villages on its west were similar to those on its east. The second time I saw it, running through neighborhoods of the capital it was a prefabricated ensemble of high concrete elements. The necessary problem of how this concrete will one day be removed was accompanied with the certainty of a *déjà vu*—that we have already seen a wall collapsed.

S

In contrast to its other side, where it could, without our even knowing, be openly denounced, directly experienced, and even painted over, where a by-now famous architectural student walked its inner perimeter and admired "the beauty of its cruelty," the Wall on our side was a highly perilous territory that was not confined to its actual physical presence. It existed throughout our country, our ideological block. For those of us not living in Berlin, the Wall was nothing but a mental and political condition rendered concrete by a physical artifact we knew existed but never saw. The eyes of its watchtowers were already built into our personalities.

H

Coming back after a few months to the olive orchard I first visited, I passed through a small breach that was still open through the construction site of the barrier line. After a ten-minute walk, I reached another series of fences, and passed again through another opening. Later I reached yet another barrier. Amongst the profusion of walls, fragments, ditches, and barbed wire that never seemed to connect, one is no longer simply either inside or outside. Long queues of people stood silently in front of roadblocks—as if disciplined by these apparatuses that seemed like doors without walls.

Talking Walls

Ines & Eyal Weizman

S

We never called it the Wall. For us it was the Antifascist Protective Rampart, our defense against the Western aggressors. The term "Wall" was strictly forbidden as it implied that the thing was directed at imprisoning rather then protecting us. We hated the Antifascist Protective Rampart for doing us such good.

H

How to describe what we see? That depends on the politics of the speaker. The wall makes one think of Berlin; the apartheid wall makes one think of South Africa; and the Israelis call it the fence, as if talking of a garden. But beyond the political semantics, the fence is paradoxically more aggressive than the wall. A fence allows the military to see through and supervise the other side. The wall is where the function of the gun is expected to be stronger than that of the eye.

S

A rumor, only recently confirmed, was that our maps were distorted by the government, confusing our sense of distance to the border, sabotaging any calculated attempt to flee over or under it. Sometimes, without a warning, in the middle of a forest we would see a simple white line painted across a narrow path. It meant stop, the border is near! Thrilled with expectation and fear, we froze, even if there were many more unpicked mushrooms on the other side. We wondered as we breathed in, was the air different there?

H

So your wall was invisible, and mine was not a wall at all.

1 Element UL 12.11 of the Berlin Wall. Berlin (photo: Heinz J. Kuzdas © 1975)

2 The prefabricated elements of the wall through Abu-Dis, near Jerusalem (photo: Eyal Weizman © 2004)

Perhaps the most invidious post-9/11 formulation I've heard from an architect is "deputizing." This was first articulated to me by an acquaintance—a distinguished urban designer—to describe the work he is doing in Washington, D.C. to help secure the city against attack. He was thrilled with the idea that the innocuous objects of everyday life could be "drafted" into use as an extension of the national defense. Thus every lamppost, newsstand, street tree, and mailbox—suitably but inconspicuously beefed-up—would become a soldier in the war on terror.

A striking instance of such deputization has just appeared across the street from my studio. A few weeks ago, a block-square federal building was suddenly surrounded by dozens of staunch-looking concrete planter boxes that now line the curb, presumably to keep al-Qaeda from driving car bombs into the lobby of the post office. I admit to a blip of ambivalence about these items. The streets surrounding the big building had been bleak and free of greenery and now we have a little bit. Alas, though, the sheriffs who appointed these deputies stopped short of providing actual trees. While a mighty oak might well stop a speeding car, the problem of terror is clearly too urgent to await the growth of saplings into a protective shield. Or perhaps they worry that Osama might hide in the leafy branches.

The self-annihilating elision of urban militarization with civic improvement is everywhere as our Orwellian administration grows increasingly free with the Big Lie as its main mode of public communication. And the local powers are eager to join in! Perhaps the most over-the-top version of the manic spinning is the so-called Freedom Tower, soon to rise at Ground Zero. What can this building possibly have to do with freedom? To get in will require a sniff from the TNT-sensitized nose of a deputized beagle, passage through banks of magnetometers, show of ID, and who knows what other biometric profiling.

Of course, there will be a further, more traditional, deterrent to freedom of access. This is, after all, not a forum for free expression and uninhibited behavior—it's an office building. Just as freedom of the press is enjoyed by those who happen to own one, so freedom of access to the Freedom Tower will be limited to those able to pay the premium rents. The "public" viewing deck atop the building will presumably also be "free" to those who pay the admission charge: Disney freedom. This must be thwarted. By aiding and abetting this paranoia, architecture and urbanism are being

Post-'9/11' planters barricade. New York (photo: Garret Linn 2005)

Deputy City

Michael Sorkin

called upon to play larger and larger roles in the project to restructure the military budget to hand off to a new set of corporate players. As the justification for the potlatch of ICBM's and battleships of the cold war wanes, a vast new apparatus of private armies, monitoring technology, and constructions are aimed at organizing citizens into the surveillable. The fortification of the nation has reverted to a medieval condition in which physical barricades assume morphological importance.

This is no way to design the city. Enshrined among our constitutional rights is freedom of assembly—the reason for cities—and the regime in Washington views it skeptically, seeing unrestricted movement and gathering as opportunities for our shadowy foes to do their worst. But it is our government that is doing its worst. As buildings and cities are increasingly deputized to play a role in their "war," we risk losing all that we are supposedly defending.

The original house in Detroit, a typical factory worker's home, perhaps an early version of the contemporary American dream house. Like many Detroit houses, it had little value—the average house value in Detroit was $24,500 (1999 report), the lowest in the nation by far, and lower than the average annual individual income of Americans. (Photo by G. Todd Roberts)

24260
The Fugitive House >>

>> Orléans, France (2001)
>> Sindelfingen, Germany (2001)
>> The Hague, The Netherlands (2002-04)
>> Hamburg, Germany (2002)
>> Karlsruhe, Germany (2003)
>> Dessau, w (2003-05)
>> Sheffield, UK (2004)
>> London, UK (2004)
>> Leipzig, Germany (2005)
>> . . .

24260 is an abandoned house from Detroit that was cut up so it could be moved and reassembled anywhere in the world. Escaping Detroit, where over 200,000 homes have been set on fire or demolished since 1960, **24260** has traveled to eight cities throughout Europe so far. Erasing its street name and keeping only the number, **24260** is a fugitive, searching for a new home.

But its survival comes with a condition. Invited for only temporary visits, it must always find another host city. Without the next invitation, **24260** will be discarded after its last residency. It is a disintegrating subject from a dysfunctional city, produced by the temporality of modernism , and discarded by modernism. A carcass of progress, dismembered from place and time, **24260** is a touring exhibition on the price of globalism.

I am 24260, standing here since the early 1920s, just inside Detroit where the suburbs begin. I am just one of the thousands of houses that are burnt but still standing, one of the tens of thousands that are empty, and one of almost two hundred thousand that were demolished. I live in a city that hardly resembles a city anymore.

I was constructed when Detroit had a chance to become the greatest city in the world. Three of the five biggest international corporations once called it their home. People from all corners of this country and from around the world came here to find good work and a new life. Houses like me were built fast and everywhere. Once the greatest manufacturing work force in this civilization lived here.

But I've been sitting empty for the last fifteen years. Now the land under me is worth more than I am. Fifteen years have passed since I last felt the stream of electricity, gas, and water run through me. In that time, I've watched the streets and the hoods get worse. I always tried to look proper and make a solid contribution to the community. I did my part.

The back end of the house was fused to test the dismantling strategy.

General deconstruction of the house in Detroit. Interior rooms and the attic floor were completely removed, keeping only the shell of the house. 2001

But the city abandoned me. It moved out to the suburbs and further, taking with it the families, jobs, and money. I've heard that about half the people of Detroit left, about one million or so. Houses that were once packed here like sardines have mostly disappeared, and now many parts of the city look like the countryside. Wild dogs and pheasants roam freely and the sidewalks and alleys are covered with wild grasses. The rumor is that you could drive an hour and not see a single soul walking around. At least it feels that way.

I have heard of ghost towns, but never a ghost city. And I would like to know what really happened to this city and why no one sleeps inside me any more. I watched plenty of my friends being burnt alive, for reasons that remain unexplained. The only fire I aim to see is one in my fireplace, to keep my people warm in the American Dream. Instead, we have Devil's Night here every year, when hundreds of houses and buildings are burnt in one night. Have people gone mad? Do they no longer believe in cities?

Every day I see trucks filled with smashed houses roar by me, but usually the demolished houses are just dumped into the basements. Houses in Detroit become their own graves.

So Detroit is not a ghost town. It is a giant 140-square-mile cemetery, full of buried houses and buildings neatly placed along the streets and sidewalks. And I could be the next. Easily.

1

But I am still strong and able, and would like to live a few more years. Sitting here is like being on death row, with demolition or incineration as my only choices. I dream about picking myself up and moving out of here, just like the people did. I would like to go somewhere where I would be wanted again. Surely there must be a place in the world where someone would love to have me as a dream house.

My luck changed a few Christmases ago, when I got a letter from the good people of Orléans, France asking me to visit. And later Sindelfingen, Hamburg, and Karlsruhe, Germany invited me too. Along the way, I have visited Dessau, Germany; The Hague; Sheffield, England; and London. I have suddenly become fashionable. I am displayed as an exhibition so that people can look at me. I like the attention that I have been getting since I left Detroit. I guess people want to find out how the most powerful economy in the world can starve its cities to the bones. And if the rest of the world wants this culture, then they can see in me the desolation at the end of modernity.

Should I make myself more dramatic and dismember myself, tear my insides out? Should I undress to expose my emptiness? Should I scream so that people will notice me, instead of passing by as if I never existed? How can I stop this drive-by history?

Nah. I should stop complaining. I am still enjoying my trip in Europe. Maybe I can see the world and never come back. Maybe a kinder and gentler city somewhere will adopt me.

>> Orléans (installed)
2001

The first reconstruction of 24260, Orléans, 2001

Students from the University of Detroit Mercy and the Academy of Design in Orléans, together with some of the staff member of *Archilab,* who have participated in the reconstruction of 24260. (photo: Daniel Pitera © 2001)

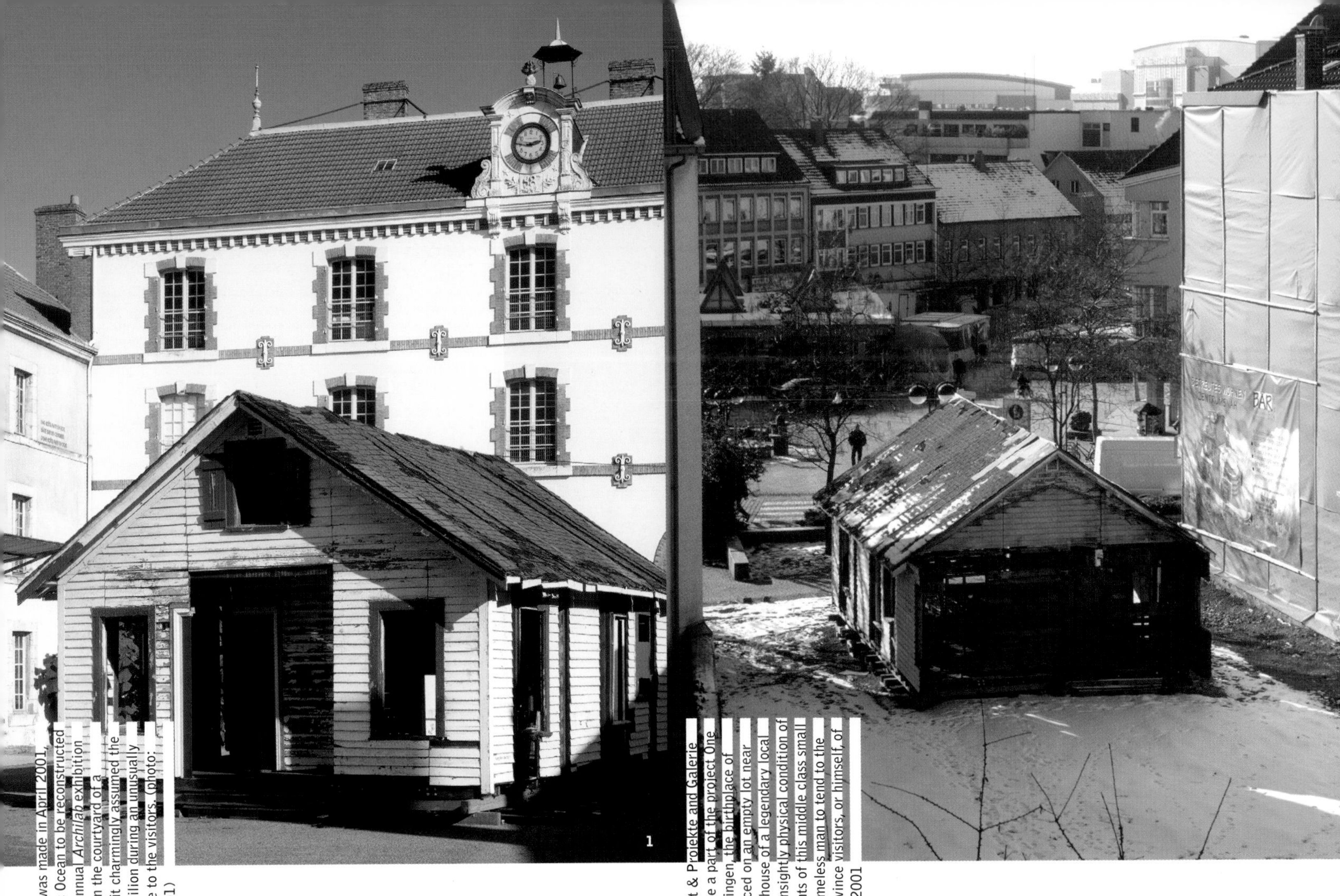

1 The first journey of 24260 was made in April 2001, when it crossed the Atlantic Ocean to be reconstructed and presented in the third annual *Archilab* exhibition in Orléans, France. Placed in the courtyard of a former military compound, it charmingly assumed the function of a temporary pavilion during an unusually hot summer, providing shade to the visitors. (photo: Courtesy of Archilab © 2001)

>> Sindelfingen (installed)

2001

2 24260 was invited by Kunst & Projekte and Galerie der Stadt Sindelfingen to be a part of the project One Site/Two Places, in Sindelfingen, the birthplace of Mercedes Benz. It was placed on an empty lot near the Marktplatz, where the house of a legendary local musician once stood. The unsightly physical condition of 24260 agitated the residents of this middle class small city, but inspired a local homeless man to tend to the house daily, perhaps to convince visitors, or himself, of the merits of decrepitude. 2001

Then, 24260 was invited to visit two different cities at the same time, so it was split into two equal parts. The back half moved to Hamburg, Germany to be displayed in the exhibition *Art & Economy* inside Deichtorhallen, a former city market. Deichtorhallen's giant industrial pitched roof that covered a 6,000-square-meter exhibition space overwhelmed 24260's tiny wooden pitched roof, suggesting the insignificance of the domestic life of a single worker against the ideology of industrial destiny. Hamburg, 2002

1 The front view, Sindelfingen. 2001

2 The back half of 24260 traveled to the Badischer Kunstverein in Karlsruhe, Germany for the exhibition *PARA > SITES: Who is moving the global city?* Lodged in the host's grandest room, it stayed warm and dry through the cold and damp winter of northern Europe. The space was darkened to simulate the bleak and lonely nights of Detroit's inner city. But the stay was brief, and it was then trucked to Dessau, Germany, a smaller, equally neglected version of industrial Detroit, for another lengthy detention. 2003

3 24260 at CIQ Square adjacent to the National Centre for Pop Music, Sheffield, England. 2004

4 24260, Deichtorhallen, Hamburg. 2002

2 The side wall of 24260, Sindelfingen. 2001

2 The back wall during its reconstruction, Orleans. 2001

>> Dessau (storaged)

2003 - 2005

>> Le Hague (storaged)
2002 - 2004

4

6

5

>> Hamburg (installed)

2002

1,3 The back half of 24260 in Deichtorhallen, Hamburg. 2002

2 The back half of 24260, Karlsruhe. 2003

4 The video *Detroit: Making It Better for You* was projected from 24260 onto the exhibition wall. Karlsruhe. 2002

>> Sheffield (installed)
2004

3

4

>> Karlsruhe (installed)
2003

1,2 Sindelfingen. 2001

3 Orléans. 2001

4 Sindelfingen. 2001

The badly decomposed front half of 24260 in storage in London. Due to its condition, the planned reunification of 24260 for the exhibition of project *Shrinking Cities* at Potsdamer Platz in Berlin—a historic site and city of reunification—was not realized. This half of 24260 is now presumed to be "dead." There is a plan to install its back half either in Leipzig or Halle in the fall of 2005.

A proposal for the Venice Architecture Biennale 2000, in collaboration with the Detroit artist Tyree Guyton. Unrealized.

Ghost on the Roof: Reincarnated Context

Jiang Jun

The Yangtse River, the artery of Chinese civilization, has recently undergone a vital surgical operation. A huge dam was inserted at the end of its bottleneck, Three Gorges, to hold back the torrent that had been running for thousands of years. The river has been turned into a bottle; the biggest reservoir on the planet.

As a direct result, the waterscape is undergoing a radical change: from a (natural) RIVER to a (man-made) LAKE, that is, from DYNAMIC to STILL. With China switching its economic pivot from the inner land to the coastline, the river that used to generate the Yangtse River Delta—a large area of naturally-made reclamation on the remote east coast—is now used to generate electricity for the east coast. The dam thus acts both as a monument and a metaphor of its demiurge: a new China moving from STILL to DYNAMIC.

Behind the overwhelmingly propagandized economic effect of the monumental act is its counteractive side effect. With the water level updated to another height, everything below—the landscape, as well as its parasitic cityscape, including 2 cities, 10 counties, and 116 towns—was systematically deconstructed and dislocated to make way for the coming transformation. The inhabitants had to move elsewhere, but there were no equivalent new cities for them. The entire authority behind the planned economy, from the high-level decision-makers to the hierarchical technical bureaucracy, was exerted to remap the topography, relocate regional productivity, and refocillate economic and social function. The bottleneck cities, which had been a silent sacrifice, were finally given a future—to rebuild themselves on the higher ground at an astronomical cost. The waterline, whose subtext is immigration line, thus demarcates the space-time between high and low, old and new, traditional and modern, dead and alive. Hydrology is hereon interpreted into anthropology; water ecology is converted into urban ecology.

The displaced population was divided into two streams. One was dispersed elsewhere as a contemporary diaspora, including the landless and jobless FLOATING population on the Golden Coast. The other was literally FLOATED to the new cities above the old cities together with their old things: furniture, electrical equipment, motorcycles, and houses. A double-layered urbanism of different characters was created. Some of the fugitive houses were privileged antiques that were officially transplanted from their original sites to new ones, dismantled and reassembled, unchanged. There was also another, more subliminal conservation: materials from the old houses—

1 The demolition of a city for the construction of the Three Gorges Dam Project. Fengjie, China (photo: Jiang Jun © 2003)

2 The dramatic stack of old and new as an urban aftermath of the Three Gorges Dam Project. ZiGui, China (photo: Jiang Jun © 2003)

roof tiles, bricks, doors, and window frames—were dislodged through massive carpet bombing, moved to the higher level with the immigrants, and reconstructed on an even higher level, the roofs of the new cities. The average height of the roofs on the new buildings was three floors. The reused materials thus created the fourth floor. A dramatic stack, an accidental hybrid, and an informal urbanism were created unconsciously. The old villages were reincarnated as the roofscape of the new city; a ghost from underwater rises above a newborn LAKE.

2

Breeding Dust

Laurent Gutierrez & Valérie Portefaix

1 In the early 1980s, the Pearl River Delta (PRD) region was transformed into a vast manufacturing hinterland for Hong Kong, as well as an experimental zone for China's new economy. Massive foreign investments from the British colony boosted a region that aspired to become the fifth Asian dragon. Established by entrepreneurs, local infrastructural projects were successfully injected with a politics of *laissez faire*. Joint ventures and private money provided the funds that allowed China to respond to the global economy and enter the World Trade Organization. The most visible trace of this recent development can be found in the form of a private highway—a 120-kilometer-long elevated strip between Shenzhen and Guangzhou. Owned by the developer Hopewell Holding and CEO Sir Gordon Wu, the Guangshen Superhighway is a unique platform which links cities and transfers merchandise from factories to the container terminals. This suggests that the configuration of this strategic network is no longer determined by local factors but by a private empire that controls the economy, the planning, and ultimately the culture of a region.

2 The enclosed dual three-lane toll expressway provides eighteen interchanges designed by Sir Gordon Wu (he is also an architect). Obviously the strategic position of these junctions increases the land value and contributes to the creation of an urban corridor that will eventually transform the PRD region into a single sprawling metropolis. At each interchange, a commercial structure was built, yet most were almost immediately left abandoned. Inspired by Le Corbusier's Plan Obus for Algiers, they were planned to accommodate a gigantic mixed-use program—commerce, office, factory, and dormitory—directly plugged into the underbelly of the infrastructure. Today, these abandoned structures are occasionally occupied by new, migrant squatters.

3 Driving at 120 kilometers per hour on the slightly congested highway—avoiding frequent car crashes, unexpected domestic animals, and crazy container-truck and bus drivers—you witness the spectacle of a devastated land undergoing massive restructuring. In between factories, dormitories, and trash areas, streams and ponds of polluted water amplify the sense of disaster, illustrating a dehumanized world. Down on the ground however, the reality is utterly different. Life carries on for a floating population of ten million people producing the "Made in China" label. Living in dormitories attached to the factories, these new migrants spontaneously appropriate the only large, sheltered space available—the superhighway.

4 A massive open market exists under the highway. Workers use this market to develop new social networks. This is not only a site for selling commodities but also for service and immediate consumption. It is a place where you can have a seat, order food, and watch a DVD on TV. With the gathering of a few chairs and the folding of a piece of fabric, a number of entertainment islands are created. The highway provides a roof, and support for lighting and electricity. In the shadow of the highway, innovative economic activities interact freely with the social pattern. Another form of energy comes from the floating condition of the land, people, TV screens, digital noise, and neon light. This hidden urbanity, which lives off the energy of a population almost entirely under the age of twenty-five, represents the necessary motor that powers the PRD region.

Underneath the Guangshen highway
Pearl River Delta region, China
(photo: Gutierrez + Portefaix © 2003)

Netting the Egnatia

A dialogue between Marina Fokidis and Lorenzo Romito

Egnatia Road is an ancient Roman road passing through the south of Italy, Albania, Macedonia, and Thrace, which was built to connect Rome and Constantinople—the Western and Eastern capitals of the divided Roman Empire. In the last century this road has seen the dramatic displacement of millions of Albanians, Armenians, Bulgarians, Greeks, Jews, Slavs, Turks, Kurds, Afghanis, and Iraqis, most notably the Greek-Turk population exchange agreed to within the 1923 Treaty of Lausanne forcing one and an half million people to leave their homeland, or the present movement of thousands of refugees and immigrants towards Western Europe. The project *Egnatia, a Journey of Displaced Memories*, seeks to collect stories of displacement, recording real accounts from those who have been forced to move along the Egnatia "corridor."

Marina Fokidis
The site in this project is no longer a point on the map but a journey, a sequence of events and actions through spaces in which the path is expressed by the meeting of the participants including producers and receivers, artists and audiences. One intention is for the project to become an archive of memories, transforming Egnatia Road into what you have been calling an "Actual Territory."[1]

Through this perception of site as a political or theoretical concept, a particular community, or an ethnographic team, architects and artists have been redefining their role into constructors of a net of human relations. What are these new sites of cultural production and how can they be studied in terms of their aesthetic expression, their communication of knowledge, and their ethical affinity?

Lorenzo Romito
Each site is itself a complex system of relations. Every attempt to observe a particular place already creates interference within this system of relations. It is the very process of observing that produces the reality itself. This means that there's no other way to comprehend than by being a participant within the reality we'd like to observe. A site's complexity in terms of relations is not objective evidence but depends on the capability of the observer him or herself, especially when dealing with non-planned and self-produced realities. We may think that these relations don't exist because we are, as observers, not capable of interpreting them. We may simply see them as chaotic reality; as something that does not make sense. But when our process of observing is empathetic

1 "Actual Territories" constitute the built city's negative—the interstitial and marginal spaces that have been abandoned or are in the process of transformation. These are the removed *lieu de la memoire*, the unconscious becoming of the urban systems, the spaces of confrontation between and contamination of the organic and the inorganic, the natural and the artificial. Here the metabolization of humanity's discarded scrap, or nature's detritus, produces a new horizon of unexplored territories that are for Stalker "Actual Territories." The term "actual" indicates the process in which space comes into being. The "actual" is not what we are, but rather that which we are becoming. From the "Stalker Manifesto," *www.stalkerlab.it.*

with the environment—even if it is extraneous to our patterns of comprehension—then we become part of its emerging relations, part of the site itself. At the same time, being outsiders and therefore detached from the observed reality, we can attempt to interpret those emergences and to communicate them.

Such situations are difficult to render intelligible because they lack connections to the present. They are to be physically witnessed rather than represented. The archive of experiences is the only possible form of mapping for these "Actual Territories." Here we are beginning to define new tools and methods to develop the self-representation of those realities, producing not projects but mostly paths and relationships.

[MF]
I remember that when we invited you to present another work entitled *Flying Carpet* in Thessalonica, Greece in 2001 you did not accept our invitation simply as such. You were happy to show your work in Greece only if we could allocate a percentage of the budget, and facilitate the organization of a road trip to the Balkan area following the path of Egnatia Road. While the work was being transported from Albania to Greece, we were physically on the road. This trip that started in Rome, passed through different places in Albania, and concluded in Greece, allowed more people to come in close touch with the changing environment to which they were exposed, giving birth to new ideas for interconnected actions and creations. The phantom of Egnatia Road, a mythic unity under which are gathered a wide variety of people and experiences, served in that case as a zone of mutual interest for fertile collaboration. The discovery of the contemporary development along the path, the conditions of this journey, and the interpersonal relations and deep involvement with the particular localities that were developed on the road constituted the base for the creation of a multicultural laboratory which is currently in process. It is true that these kind of cultural productions still cannot be executed outside institutional circumstances but they are not, any longer, determined by them.

Various kinds of collaborations emerge in diverse locations involving in a horizontal hierarchy the initiators, the public (which usually consists of the observed communities), the postproduction

An open 'black' market. Albania, 2005

team, and the institution itself. Although such endeavors do not often survive commercialization in the contemporary art market, their value does not rely on an object but on the interaction between the participants. Just how can one determine the nature of collaboration in such ephemeral situations? Do receivers and producers adopt truly interchangeable roles? How can one measure the ethical affinity of an art practice that moves away from being an aesthetic intervention and becomes more of a public service?

[LR]

It's a process where producer and receiver play a common game; that's the reason why we never conceived of Stalker as a group but as an interrelated open system which is growing and emerging through its actions and through all the individuals that operate with (for and among) Stalker. A reality without one physical body. "We" has always been an entity that comprises "others," who, without pretending to be us, participate together in the activities becoming "us" in their/our actions.

In this way Stalker could be anyone. Stalker is a desiring community where no one belongs and where individuals encounter each other. It is an unstable entity, a temporary community founded on possibilities, on desire, on intention, on promise, and waiting. Such desiring power is Stalker's hypothesis: "transgressive excitement, tension in motion, energetic investment in the future." Stalker will always generate dissipation of energies, drawing a dynamic vital geometry in order to make this power come to life without any determination.

By "coming to life" it generates a space which is an ethical, political, and aesthetic space; a real, autonomous, living space; a territory— made up of environments, situations, and places which have been removed from chaos, from idle and ratified dominions—that is finding its way from destruction and destructors, and re-establishing a creative circularity which has been taken from us by the transformation of life into merchandise. This is Stalker's necessary ethical, political, and aesthetic approach. Without these premises, Stalker's games run the risk of becoming fixed games.

Sign on East Warren, near East Grand Boulevard. 2002

Words, Images, and Spaces: A Language for a New City?

A workshop, installation, and video,
Near eastside Detroit (2002)

Words, Images, and Spaces (W.I.S.)
A Language for a New City?

Inspired by an anonymous street sign with the word "Economy" that pointed towards nothing, **iCUE** posted eighteen signs with different words on telephone poles and empty houses, and created a new floor for a building using reconditioned wood scavenged from demolished houses. Not believing that only corporate redevelopment or the suburbs could save the inner city, these temporary installations honor the personal inventions and community works that have nurtured Detroit. While hinting at gentrification and displacement ahead, W.I.S. imagines if a new city could be borne out of these words, images, and spaces.

IMAGE 1

IMAGE 2

IMAGE 3

FORWARD
MEMORY
CREATE
COMMUNITY
FUTURE
IMAGINE
DREAM
CONSTRUCT
INSPIRE
UTOPIA
WILL
EVOLVE
SUSTAIN
ECONOMY
VISIONS
PROTECT
ECOLOGY
TRUTH

Construct
A collapsed building on Chene Street, just south of Fisher Freeway and the General Motors Cadillac Assembly Plant. Chene Street was once a very vibrant commercial street within what came to be known as Poletown, a community of Polish immigrants. The assembly plant was built in the early 1980s, promising to bring thousands of jobs to a city that was in desperate need of economic and tax bases. Despite strong protests by residents, and national media attention on the plight of citizens under the coercion of corporations and city government—the Coleman Young administration—about four thousand homes were destroyed to make room for a symbolic return of the car industry to Detroit. The trickle-down theory of American urban and economic policy obviously failed, in a dramatic fashion, as the decline of Chene Street instead accelerated.

"You walk by here everyday, and that block is about to fall on somebody´s head at any minute. And you watch, you watch. That´s bad, man. That needs to be removed. You know what I am saying. These kids go to Campbell elementary school and that block right on top there is about to fall [on them walking under]. I am telling you. You see it. Its gonna come down man."
Otis

Forward
Former Packard Automobile Plant, on East Perry and Canton Streets. What was once the source and blood of the community has now become the wound, from which the destruction of the urban fabric seems to spread. Most of the houses around the plant were built by the Packard Corporation to provide housing for its workers. But the abandoned automobile plant now forms an apocalyptic background to the community that is literally burning.

"I remember when this whole neighborhood was full of houses. It used to be more productive back then, but over the period of time everything just diminished."
A home owner

Ecology
John's Blues Club, an informal entertainment joint, at Saint Aubin near Farnsworth Street. We felt the sign "Ecology" was most appropriate here, where the carpet was recycled to good use. The sign found a good home and may stay there for some time.

"I don't know what happend. NO. You tore them down [the houses] and people move from here. Long time ago. Ive been here so long I don't remember."
Grandma

"Inspire? Well. Its all about the magic word. What's the magic word? That everyone wants."
"Love?"
"L.O.V.E. You got it right."
Jimmy C.

Visions
An open field at East Canfield and Russell Streets. One may wonder if the lack of population and jobs is the only reason for the current state of Detroit. What could be the vision of Detroit—a city built in the twentieth century—in this new century?

"Hey man. I am gonna represent, represent. I represent, represent, represent, E.S.P. Down South, M.S.P.E.E. and don't blame me. Cause I am a player. Represented. Alright. I am out."
A kid at Mt. Elliot and Perry Streets.

Image boards,
Chene Street, near East Warren.
Photographs of agriculture, transportation, recycling, water, and other references to this landscape and its potential were placed in three different locations. We imagined that these images could help to visualize the words that we posted.

A demolished house
Chene and East Forest Streets.
Very often demolished houses are never removed. In some cases, electricity or natural gas was never properly shut off, making it too dangerous to remove the houses. In other cases, the reasons are unknown. We began collecting wood that was accessible and usable from demolished houses at six different sites, and recycled it to build a functional structure in the near eastside.

A recycling center for building material, School of Architecture, University of Detroit Mercy.
Scavenged lumber was recycled and sanded to a usable condition. Can the same intention be applied to recycle a city?

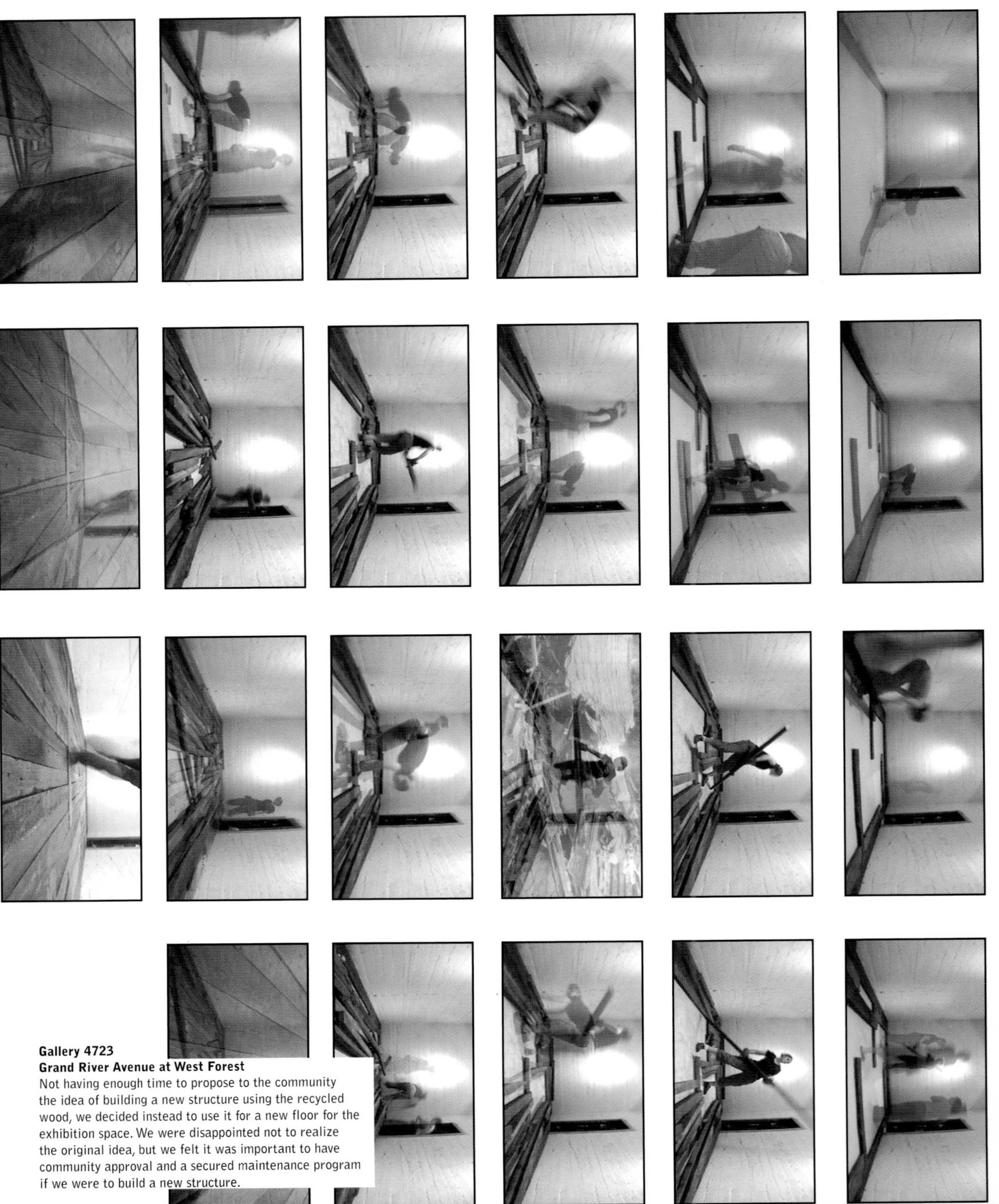

Gallery 4723
Grand River Avenue at West Forest
Not having enough time to propose to the community the idea of building a new structure using the recycled wood, we decided instead to use it for a new floor for the exhibition space. We were disappointed not to realize the original idea, but we felt it was important to have community approval and a secured maintenance program if we were to build a new structure.

If we acknowledge that there is something like the experience of urban time, the urban transformation of East Germany, the former German Democratic Republic, since the fall of the Wall could be described as one of radical rupture and contradiction in time rather than as a continuous evolutionary flow. The German reunification by no means remained a mere political act, but became a practice of enormous social and institutional dimensions, which replaced or substituted not only habits, experiences, values, and most importantly personnel in an unexpectedly short time, but which also transformed and replaced the socialist city.

A peculiar phenomena after the collapse of the socialist regime was that the very same streets, houses, courtyards, and monuments that had once formed the invisible and amicable backdrop of East Germans' daily life, suddenly seemed to them embarrassingly dilapidated, gray, and dirty. The whole city in its deplorable state was suspected of having engraved the ideology of state socialism into its very look and built fabric. Arguably, it wasn't the opening of the Berlin Wall, but the adoption of a new Western gaze that embodied the very moment that collapsed the East and its urbanism. The cultural transformation started not with the laying or removing of the first brick, but with a different way of seeing.

In a gigantic process of urban renovation the meanings of and familiarity with the recent past were replaced by another earlier past. Formerly broken or lost historicist decorations—elaborate sculptures, roofs, and spires—were quickly replaced, creating a pristine nineteenth-century charm that suggests bourgeois wealth in a post-industrial/post-socialist reality of unemployment and migration.

The surprisingly fashionable rewriting of city guides in the late '90s tried to catch up with the changed appearance of these East German cities. A particular type of photographic seeing has been used, which depicts on two opposing pages one and the same place *before* and *after* the political transformation. Viewed from the same photographic perspective, formerly derelict historical and socialist buildings are weighed against their renovated, candy-colored versions. The oppositions present an ideological critique that is clearly intended as a reproach against the immediate past.

Stereoscopic Times

Ines Weizman

The recurrence of this method of representation in German history makes the use of this technique paradigmatic for ideological shifts and major political changes. It represents not only the physical transformation of the same place differentiated by time, but also a radical break with the immediate past and a completely new set of ideals. What you believed in *before* becomes a crime *after*.

Nineteenth-century pairs show the replacement of medieval buildings with modern bourgeois ones; post-World War II sets of images show the old city versus its rubble; 1960s images boast clean well-serviced social housing blocks versus the almost derelict and dilapidated nineteenth-century fabric; and contemporary images show now again, newly reconstructed Prussian-style architecture, thus (for the time being) closing the century-and-a-half-long cycle of dialectical before and after. But in the case of present-day East Germany the representation and reading of urban time has been dyslexic. The renovated building puts us back in time. Staging an amazing coup, it is the initial *before*—the nineteenth century—that has managed to place itself both before and after the *after*—the twentieth century. In contrast to the linear understanding of urban history as a complex accumulation of physical artifacts and an evolution of a variety of styles, the "reorganization" of urban time discussed above meant that urban time was now chopped up into conflicting and alienated pockets of ideological and political tempo-localities.

View towards St Nicolas in 1986 ...
... and after its renovation in 1999. Leipzig, Germany
(images taken from: *Leipzig. Den Wandel zeigen*, Edition Leipzig, 2000)

Theme City

Minsuk Cho

One of a number of dynamically developing Asian "wonder cities," Seoul was caught in a whirlwind of constant transformation, with the swarms of people softening its rapid and brutal construction. This form of urbanism appeared infallible due to the sheer density and consequent vitality that mass generates regardless of quality. Under the magic umbrella of density, any type of architecture worked. Mass served to reflexively support the national sentiment of "living well is the best revenge" by creating a densely populated modern city as the prime collective therapy for the post-war trauma of the latter half of the twentieth century.

Then toward the late '90s everything in Korea changed. The insatiable snowball of economic prosperity came to an abrupt halt. The International Monetary Fund bailout struck a vicious blow to Korea's seemingly indomitable post-war optimism, and for the first time in modern Korean history negative economic growth was recorded.

And just as Korea comes close to finally reaching its national goal of one dwelling per nuclear family - after decades of creating millions of apartment units per year mostly in new satellite sleeping cities - the urban explosion has come to a sudden halt. The urban mass is moving in previously unexperienced and unimagined directions. Suddenly, renovation, remodeling, and redevelopment are the most frequently used words in the construction industry, referring to interior spaces, buildings, cities, and even to the nation. Green spaces, the ecology, and culture are new objectives as Korea begins to redefine what it means to be a modern society. For instance, the initial 3.4 kilometer stretch of Korea's first elevated high-speed road that cut through the heart of Seoul was demolished in 2003 to restore a river covered over by the infrastructure invasion thirty years ago. This is but one step in the harsh, painful process of coming to the realization that being modern does not necessarily mean growing bigger and adding more TV channels, cineplexes, shopping malls, or avenues lined with rows of skyscrapers designed by famous corporate American architecture firms. Adding quality is the new solution.

Theme City–Paju Book City/Heyri Art Valley

Theme cities are a recent urban experiment in Korea, reflecting a major shift in the political climate in the last decade. The construction of modern Seoul has been mainly associated with an era of centralized power, with the happy marriage between a military dictatorship and a few *chaebols* (corporate conglomerates) managing the whole country from the '60s until the early '90s, with an "Asian-style" economic development strategy. This was a time when thinking big was the only way to satisfy the ever-increasing demand for space unimagined before in this country.

The new theme cities are based on painfully and gradually gained democratic freedom and the democratized government's will to decentralize its power. They also coincided with economic inertia. From their inception less than ten years ago, two utopian-tinged urban/semi-urban developments located forty kilometers north of Seoul and ten minutes drive from the border between South and North Korea, Paju Book City and Heyri Art Valley, with their community-based, ecologically conscious, and controlled development, clearly positioned themselves as an alternative to Seoul where chaotic/dynamic urban qualities are generated accidentally by an uncontrollable market economy system.

These new cities were developed by unions of relatively small companies (*paju*: publishing companies) or groups of people with shared interests (*heyri*: artists and people engaged with cultural production) instead of being conducted by large construction and development firms. As their names imply, theme cities were initially devoted to specific industries and interests: Heyri Art Valley for instance primarily includes artists' studios, galleries, movie studios, and other cultural facilities; whereas Paju Book City, designated as an industrial zone, caters to the publishing industry with several publishing houses, a distribution center, a convention hall, and other supporting facilities.

This experiment has been lead by unions and groups of architects composed of many individuals who are active in the ongoing decision-making process. In a country where the process of planning new cities for millions has been a rampant exercise of political and economic power by the few, the process of making this new type of small city has been a way of practicing the newly-improved democracy.

Contact Zone Colors

Hans Ulrich Obrist in conversation with Anri Sala

Hans Ulrich Obrist: Could you tell me a little about the project (in Tirana, Albania)?
Anri Sala: Well it's been going on for a year. Edi Rama has been mayor of Tirana for the last two years. This has been a time of large transformations in the city. In some of these transformations, color has played a role in the changing of the city, and parts of the town have literally been covered with color. It's very much about the relationship between the given context and the political decisions taken in order to change the situation and improve the quality of life in the city.

[HUO]: It's like Mayakovsky during the Russian Revolution—the city is a palette.
[AS]: The relationship between the city and its inhabitants is made up by the quality of the services that the city offers. In a city that offers good public services people feel valued and in their turn look after the city. In Tirana, things have not been like this. But now that there is a possibility for change, there is no money for big transformations and until recently there was no hope that one day life in the city could be better. But there is need for change; there is an emergency. I think Edi is bringing hope and infrastructure at the same time. What he's doing affects both the emotional life of the people and the way they use the city. In the beginning, he wasn't sure whether the color project was working, so he organized a poll with two questions. The first one was do you like the color thing? Sixty percent said they liked it and forty percent no. And then the second question was do you want it to continue, and ninety percent said yes and only ten percent said no.

[HUO]: Your intention revolves around the notion of change and transformation. A key question is how a city can be transformed. One solution is through architecture, such as through the museum in Bilbao, a new business district, or symbol. Here it is very different. So would you say that color is cheap?
[AS]: In Tirana color is concentrated on those parts of the city that have no other chances. They are now under colors. In a way what is being done with the color in the city is a kind of violation, but for the first time in its history it is a positive violation. In a city that has always been violated, that is significant. Another thing to understand, especially as the project is going to be included in the Utopia Station, is that what is happening there is not a model for other cities.

1,3 A typical newly-painted social housing block, Tirana, Albania. 2005

2 A typicalt unpainted social housing block, Tirana, Albania. 2005

2

[HUO]: As a mayor, he also has an incredible possibility to define the notion of a museum of the twenty-first century. The whole museum discussion is so stuck right now. After the idea of the expansion of the museum, there was a shrinking of the museum, but really it is still just variations on one model of the museum. There are so many other models that could be possible.
[AS]: In our last conversation we talked about the idea of Tirana being a living museum. It will be good when other artists are included in the project of coloring—at the moment it's only him. He hopes the current project will reach a kind of harmony—not in terms of colors, but in terms of relations between outdoors and indoors, so that in the future it won't be remembered as the city of colors but rather as a city of signals, where the colors won't be there as a dressing but they will be as organs.

Hotel Neustadt

Matthias Rick

The project *Hotel Neustadt*, in Halle-Neustadt, Germany, was created during the summer of 2003 as an initiative of the Thalia Theatre Halle. A socialistic town vision developed in the '70s for one hundred thousand inhabitants, Halle-Neustadt has lost half of its residents since the German unification in 1989. The ninety-two room Hotel Neustadt was a temporary experiment in which the urban emptiness of Halle-Neustadt was defined as a theatrical realm. For the project, one of four empty tower blocks was transformed into a hotel, which was planned, equipped, and designed by more than one hundred teenagers. During the time *Hotel Neustadt* was open—from the end of August to the beginning of October 2003—2,952 overnight stays were made.

Hotel Neustadt was also an international festival, with 23 contributions by 153 international artists and the Thalia Theatre that dealt with city shrinkage, life in a tower block, life in a hotel, and the integration of the neighbors. The cooperation between architecture and theater created a possibility to change urban rules and to establish new forms of communication.

The Slide For Hotel Neustadt

Video, 03.27 minutes
Halle, Neustadt, Germany (2003)

THE SLIDE is a continuous transparent tube that descends eighteen floors from the top to the bottom of an empty hi-rise building in Halle Neustadt. Visitors can ride inside **THE SLIDE** on a specially-designed sled, flying through the walls, floors, and ceilings, and even outside of the building. **THE SLIDE** is a new kind of entertainment that combines the reality and fiction of architecture, and is ideal for so many empty buildings in East Germany.

"Hey Mom and Dad. I went through a building today!"

The abandoned center of Halle-Neustadt with *Hotel Neustadt* in front.
(photo: Hedi Lusser © 2003)

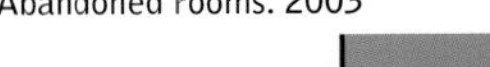

Abandoned rooms. 2003

The teenagers decided to give every floor its own atmosphere and every room its own theme: jungle-room, autumn-room, ocean-room.
(photos: Matthias Rick © 2003)

In a summer workshop, the teenagers built furniture and lamps, created wallpapers, and worked with textiles. Beds, shelves, desks, benches, interior design elements, and art installations were made using wooden doors from abandoned buildings as the main building material.
(photo: raumlabor berlin © 2003)
(photo: Benjamin Foerster-Baldenius © 2003)
(photo: Annett Jumrich © 2003)

"Yes you are absolutely correct. **THE SLIDE** saved Halle Neustadt. Before **THE SLIDE**, the town was loosing people. People were moving out to more exciting cities. Now Halle Neustadt is the most exciting city in Saxony, may be even the whole Germany. People are not just visiting and touring Halle Neustadt, but they want to live here too. We may have to build more housing now, because there is waiting lines for apartments and houses here now. I just can't believe it. It's the best thing happened to this city, may be in our history."

We designed and built the espresso bar, where hotel guests could have their breakfast and where ideas were exchanged on how to make the hotel work and how to run this temporary city.
(photo: raumlabor_berlin © 2003)
(photo: Syntosil © 2003)

The hotel had a complete infrastructure. Teenagers operated the reception, and guests picked up fresh linen from the linen room.
(photo: Gert Kiermeyer © 2003)
(photo: Matthias Rick © 2003)

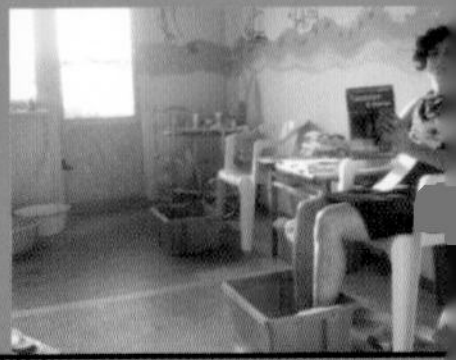

"We should stop tearing down empty buildings from now on. Imagine. Every town in East Germany could have THE SLIDE."

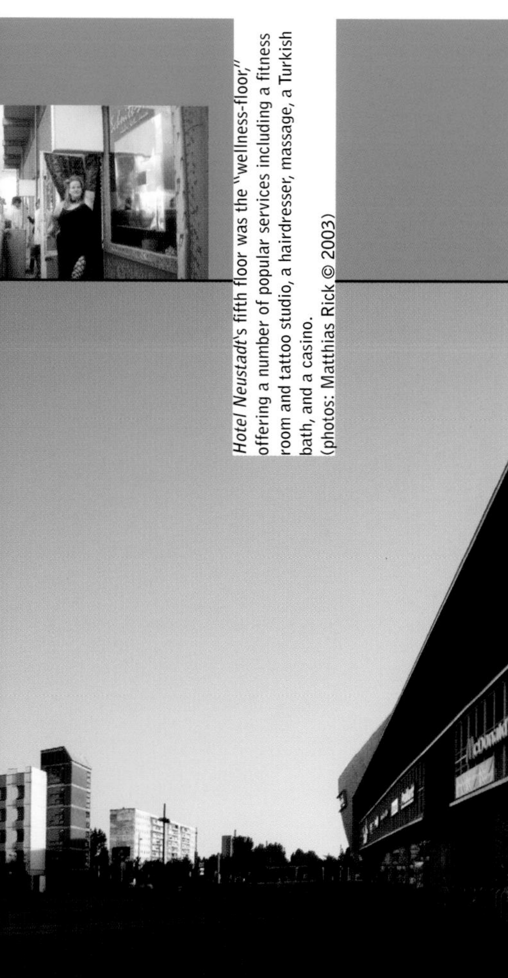

Hotel Neustadt's fifth floor was the "wellness-floor," offering a number of popular services including a fitness room and tattoo studio, a hairdresser, massage, a Turkish bath, and a casino.
(photos: Matthias Rick © 2003)

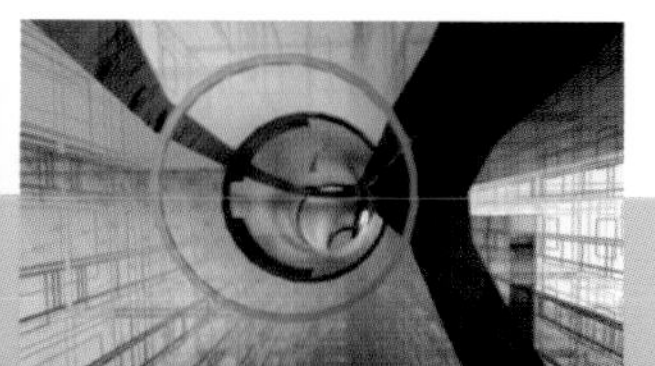

A Temporary City

People are amazed that I have been Halle Neustadt so often. The reaction is the same to my trips to Detroit. It seems that no one else goes to the places I visit.

Halle Neustadt and Detroit are two places most people want leave, especially if they are young and educated. In Germany, hopes were high that reunification would bring people from the west to the east. But that did not happen as more than 1.2 million people left the east, even though 500,000 new houses were built there. Instead, the economic and infrastructural upgrading of the east created many ironies, like the "illuminated meadows"[1]—pure infrastructural systems without any buildings—which have sprouted upon a landscape of twenty percent urban depopulation and fifteen percent unemployment.

With the economy more fluid and mobile than ever, it's futile to try to prevent labor and capital from leaving any place, not just East Germany. And it's not only people that are moving but also cities[2] and even nations[3]. Instead of trying to return to a once glorious state, cities like Detroit and Halle Neustadt must reinvent themselves to exist in a condition of movement rather than stasis. It is not enough to keep people from abandoning a place. This must be supplemented by creating an environment that will attract people to the place.

In this respect, *Hotel Neustadt* started with the right question: what could bring people to a city that everybody wants to leave. Even though the hotel was temporary—only for two months—it did create the conditions for people to come to Halle Neustadt, changing the direction of social movements. Designed and renovated by local teenagers, this full- and extra-service hotel occupied the first eight floors of an eighteen-floor abandoned dormitory building from the German Democratic Republic. It was enhanced with a balcony mall, that featured a wellness shop, a hair salon, a miniature golf course, and a casino, in addition to a performing art center for modern theater and rap battles, an independent cinema, a city tour, a tourist bureau, a gift shop, a rent-a-bike public transportation center, a public park with an outdoor sauna facility, a recreational center for BMX and skate boards, a communal cafeteria, an espresso bar with a dance floor, a breakfast bar, sporting festivals for extreme sports, outdoor performance spaces, a lecture hall, an underground night club, and more. This hotel-city was so complete that there was no need to go anywhere else. It was a city without a master plan, a new city within a dying city, a temporary city within a long-term city, a nomadic city within a static one. The hotel brought the missing elements to Halle Neustadt. Even the mayor and the council members of Halle stayed overnight at *Hotel Neustadt*.[4]

Hotel Neustadt circumvented ordered studies and planning and plunged into the self-generating capacity of informal urban strategies that thrive on participatory interaction between artists and the populace, outsiders and locals, and bottom-up and top-down movements. Resembling a high-rise favela, *Hotel Neustadt* also questioned the technocracy, or the appearance, of urban order in a nation that is struggling to maintain its economic standards. The recycling of abandoned GDR materials, such as hundreds of doors, beds, furniture, bed sheets, towels, utensils, and other institutional and domestic products, to fix, furnish, and operate the hotel incubated the idea of reinventing the existing in the face of obsolescence.

And this returns to the reason why I go to Detroit and Halle Neustadt. It is to see the fault lines of modernist cities, from which something new is beginning to emerge—ideas and designs that are fresh and rebellious, like the new growth that miraculously pushes up from the cracking sidewalks and falling buildings of decaying cities.

1 "Illuminated meadows" is an expression ironically used in East Germany for vacancies in newly developed industrial estates. They are the sobering counter-image of the promised "flourishing landscapes" since the majority of the investments are not visible on-site. An illuminated meadow is pure infrastructure without any buildings. It consists of a circulation system (roads and parking lots), utilities, and an extended or newly built sewage treatment plant. In the Halle-Leipzig region, illuminated meadows document, on the one hand, failed financial assistance policies, and on the other hand, false growth predictions and real estate speculation in the first half of the 1990s. In reference to Rochus Wiedemer, "Why demolitions?" *Project Shricking Cities*, Berlin. 2004

2 Metropolitan Detroit is one of the best examples of a moving city, as Detroit continues to be abandoned while the suburbs are successively expanding, following a radial centrifugal movement of the built environment over time and space.

3 With the population of many Western European states declining dramatically from aging and low birth rates, the reduction of their productive population could lead to an inability to maintain the current level of economy, infrastructure, and services. An inevitable remedy for the problem of shrinking nations is immigration. Since most of the immigrant population of Western Europe is from colonial territories—past or present—the dominant states become dependent on the subordinate states. Soon, there could be competition between dominant states to attract population from subordinate states, offering residency and citizenship as was done before. As their populations become minorities, the dominant nations may have to give up their territories to the subordinate nations. This reversed colonization, along with the process of globalization due to trade, foreign investment, or outsourcing of labor, industries, and technology, could erode the validity of the nation-state.

4 Halle Neustadt had a mayor during the GDR period but is now governed from Halle.

There was a mobile sauna on Neustadt Square. For the first time in Neustadt's forty-year history, people ran around naked, bathed in ice cold water, cut wood with power saws, or talked to each other over a beer. We brought life to the square, late into the night.
(photo: Matthias Rick © 2003)
(photo: Gert Kiermeyer © 2003)

In the abandoned main hall of a train station next to the hotel, we organized rap-battles for the teenagers. It was used every evening as a refectory for the hotel operators. (photos: Matthias Rick © 2003)

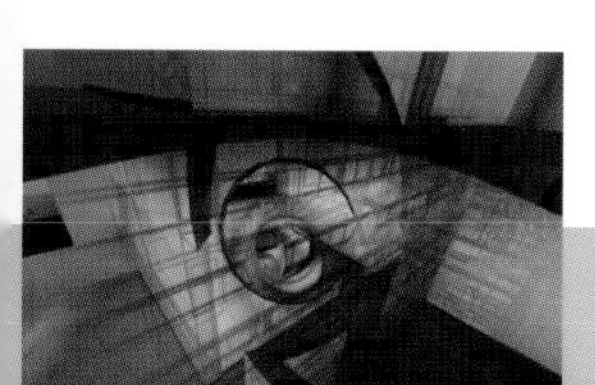

"I've been waiting for something like this for a long time. It's boring to take my date to movies and restaurants all the time. Now I can take him to THE SLIDE."

There was also a tourist information booth, run by teenagers, from which you could rent bikes or get a guided city tour through Halle-Neustadt.
(photo: Annett Jumrich © 2003)
(photo: Benjamin Foerster-Baldenius © 2003)

The gigantic four hundred-meter-long train platform was cleaned daily through Refuge Shelter of the Future, a performance by the Austrian group Club Real.

Grotest Maru, a performance group from Berlin, staged street theater on Neustadt Square during the opening of the festival.
(photo: Annett Jumrich © 2003)

"I was going so fast, I couldn't believe it. And so smooth too."

During the festival the Hotel also featured the international hotel movie festival *Rent a Fiction*. An installation by the Swiss group Syntosil created a state of disorientation as an experience. (photos: Matthias Rick © 2003)

For their project *Balcony Tuning*, the Berlin architects Peanutz gave suggestions to the residents of Neustadt on how to improve their living spaces. (photo: peanutz-architekten © 2003)

From Buenos Aires came the architectural collective m777. They developed *Social Lottery*, a possibility to change one's personal destiny for a day. (photo: Annett Jumrich © 2003)

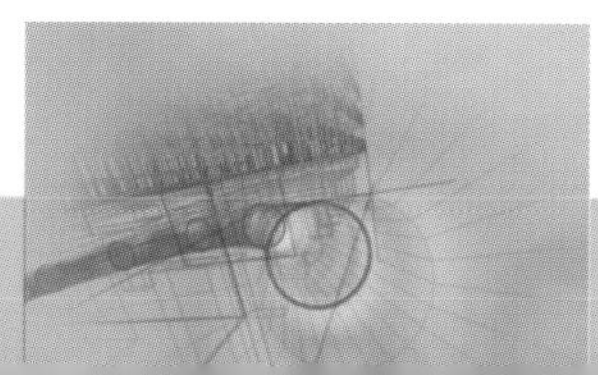

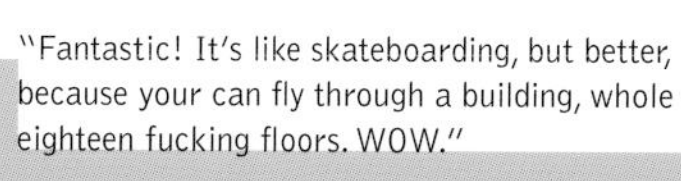

"Fantastic! It's like skateboarding, but better, because your can fly through a building, whole eighteen fucking floors. WOW."

Most spectacular was Sportification, a space-reclaiming strategy organized by the Complizen group in Halle, which provided a day of alternative and sports activities including the tower-block Frisbee race, BMX ride-down-the-stair competition, free-form climbing of the hotel facade, the first balcony triathlon, and the freestyle BMX bike course, built out of abandoned wooden doors by the architectural office raumlabor_berlin.
(photos: Annett Jumrich © 2003)

(photo: Benjamin Foerster-Baldenius © 2003)

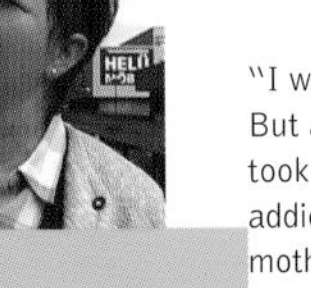

"I was worried that my kids would get hurt. But after seeing how safe the design was, I took the slide myself. I am now THE SLIDE addict. I can't wait until I can take my mother and father to THE SLIDE when they visit me next week."

[1] Quoted after Oliva Henkel and Karsten Wolff. *Berlin Underground Techno und Hip Hop zwischen Mythos und Ausverkauf* (Berlin: 1996), 32.

In the twentieth century, Berlin was an urban laboratory for examining the residual. The collapse of four German states, the destruction of World War II, the division of the city, stagnation, bad planning, and deindustrialization created spaces which were deprived of their normal cycle of economic use as well as the everyday life of the city's population. In this way seemingly functionless spaces were created which formed a breeding ground for unexpected activities—from gardens, trailer camps, markets, sport, and recreation to cultural activities and nightlife. Along with these, new fashions, cultures, and lifestyles were created. While in the '70s and early '80s followers of the squatters' movements, alternative lifestyles, and punk experimented with collective forms of living and subversive aesthetics, after the fall of the Berlin Wall in 1989 a club culture and techno scene developed which reflected the emerging euphoria and brought forth a new art and music scene.

A good example of this is UFO, the first techno disco of the period before the fall of the Berlin Wall. As an illegal club it informed its patrons through telephone chains and eluded the police by continually moving. "The concept of UFO was simple. It took off and landed somewhere," says Dimitri Hegemann, the initiator of UFO. Many clubs copied this concept, always looking for new, unusual locations. By using music equipment, strobe lights, fog machines, drinks, and drugs, unusual places could be transformed in just a few hours into the most sought-after club spaces. It was even easier to install one of the legendary weekday bars, which were only open one day a week. And to avoid the risk of petrification, established venues developed the principle of a club in a club, each of which has its own program and appeals to a different audience. By means of this principle, change that is no longer present in external circumstances is maintained. Instability becomes the motor of constant new discovery.

Temporary activities create a maximum of intensity with a minimum of substance. Existing infrastructures, buildings, and land reserves are activated with the most meager local resources. This ease allows investors without capital to actively design the city and its space. The basic rules of capitalism seem to be without power in these zones: cultural and urban experiments can be realized practically without financial means and then in the process often develop an enormous effectiveness.

The Ephemeral

Philipp Oswalt

Through temporary activities, transformer stations, bunkers, and coal stores are made into places of recreation; supermarkets and administrative offices are transformed into art galleries; factory buildings into apartments and cultural centers. As in a surrealist collage, elements of opposite worlds meet, creating crossovers of different cultural areas that had previously been separated. The basis of this is the club that serves as a platform for different programs. The same applies for the club interiors where materials and objects from extremely disparate contexts find a common meeting ground. In this way, a space for dealing with rejected, excluded aesthetics is created: while the aesthetics of the German Democratic Republic have been systematically eliminated in the official Berlin of the `90s, the club and art scene has critically appropriated them by recycling found material.

The principle of crossovers also has an effect on social categories. The "Polish Markets" which appeared in West Berlin at the end of the `80s were places where Poles, Turks, and Germans encountered each other with an otherwise unknown intensity and directness. Another example of social mixture is *Volxgolf*, organized by a private initiative on the grounds of the former Stadium of World Youth. Construction workers, managers, refugee children, the downtown scene from Mitte, and Turks from Wedding meet here to play golf, now and again playing at night with fluorescent balls, barbecue fires, and beer.

Due to their instability, temporary uses usually exist for only a transitional period at a location, but they often act as triggers that enable a more permanent use to establish itself. For instance, of the slightly more than five hundred homes in Berlin that were occupied by squatters in the `80s and `90s, about two-thirds were emptied, but the remaining one-third could be given a lasting use by purchasing or renting. These houses today form a network of alternative culture. Another example is the exhibition *37 Rooms*, which took place for one week in the summer of 1992 in various empty buildings. This one-time art event was a sort of trial run for the twenty-odd commercial galleries that are now located in these spaces.

Established institutions such as museums and marketing departments of large corporations are copying the nomadic strategies and event character of temporary uses in an attempt to push their way into the youth and culture scene. They stage street events such as the Street Soccer World Cup in 1995 in the Lustgarten on Museum Island in Berlin which was organized by the sporting goods company Puma as part of an advertising campaign.

The temporary in Berlin is thus in danger of becoming established or being "taken over by the enemy." At the same time, new activities are being created in residual zones located somewhat further out. Here the leftover energy of the metropolis can be released and "free radicals" can develop. Contrary to the lethargy of architecture and the ossification of buildings, temporary activities are flexible and changeable in their fleeting lightness. As persistent and unpredictable as temporary activities are, they will undoubtedly continue to spring up unexpectedly in the future of the city.

Polish Market in Potsdamer Platz, Berlin (photo: Karsten Burkert © 1989)

The Yaam Club

Elke Knöß & Wolfgang Grillitsch

In 1995 the open-air club Yaam occupied an abandoned industrial site, opposite the eastern harbor, at the Spree River in the Treptow area of Berlin. This appropriation of city space made a formerly non-accessible area available to the public. The Yaam is a non-profit organisation that does not receive any financial aid from the government, with twenty-five to thirty-five active and passive members.

Through its great variety of music and sports events, market stands with food, clothes, hairdressers, palm readers, a kids corner—where children can play and are supervised—and other events and programs, it attracted a big public and even provides a number of jobs. Because several youth clubs had closed in the area, the Yaam naturally provided social work programs for so-called "problematic teenagers and children" by engaging them in sport and music events.

The open-air site, surrounded by industrial buildings and the river bank, worked simultaneously as dance floor, bar, play and sportsgrounds, skatescape, beach, market, kindergarten, and public kitchen. The club opens on Saturday and Sunday afternoons in spring, summer, and autumn. In one afternoon it can attract up to two thousand people, of every age and from many different nations. The Yaam is a very special multicultural space, which is unique in Berlin.

With no budget, using found materials and objects and the volunteer work from its club members, the site was furnished and established. In summer 1996, the Yaam organised a game called *A Trip to Jamaica*. The participants had to skate; play various games that were designed like giant puzzles; row down the river; climb up a tower; and ride a steel cable that stretched fifty-eight meters over an open area, collecting objects while gliding six meters high. The winner got a paid trip to Jamaica.

Peanutz was asked to design and construct the cable railway. Through this planning process, we began to ask for building permission from the city, not just for the cable railway, but also for the game and the whole club. We started to do a survey of the site, and talked to the fire brigade, various building and environmental engineers, and civil servants. We had to restructure certain parts of the club and finally received permission to build and use the site as a club and public space. This is how the Yaam Club became a legal institution.

1 **Yaam's *Chillscape* on sunday afternoon (photo: Boris Geilert © 1996)**

2 **Soundsystem on an old trailer with Yaam resident DJ Olli Massive (photo: Boris Geilert © 1996)**

3 **Floorpainting of a minigolf course by Jim Avignon. Yaam was the first place in Berlin where streetball was established. (photo: Boris Geilert © 1996)**

4 **The Yaam is a place, where everybody can show off his skills and get respect for them. (photo: Boris Geilert © 1996)**

2

3

4

In 1997 the Yaam Club had to leave the Treptow site and moved a few hundred meters down the river to the Kreuzberg section of Berlin. This place was also an abandoned industrial space with a big open-air site and three former storage buildings. The club started with a three-day celebration, the DJ Culture Festival. We got permission to use not just the open-air site, but also the industrial halls as a club. Again, the place was furnished with found objects and materials and the help of many club members. We planned three stages—one open-air and the others in two industrial halls—markets, indoor and outdoor skatescapes, several sport fields, and many bars. We have also designed a beach at the Spree riverbank.

The Club members of the Yaam are *bricoleurs* as Claude Lévi-Strauss described in *The Savage Mind*. They have managed to make the necessary things work with little expenditure. Through the process of *bricolage* they have created their own style of designing the place. Our work as architects and urban designers was to negotiate between the *bricoleurs* and the local authorities. We are the architectural and urban lawyers for the Yaam Club. In 1999 the Yaam moved back to its first site in Treptow. Then in October 2004 they occupied a place on the other side of the Spree River, where they hopefully can stay some months. The Yaam Club depends on abandoned sites, which are becoming less available these days.

5 During the DJ CultureFestival, many sport contests took place on the big "half pipe," where skaters, skate boarders, and BMX riders competed for different games.
(photo: Mathias Schormann © 1997)

6 Eight thousand people visited the Yaam Club during DJ Culture Festival 1997.
(photo: Boris Geilert © 1997)

7 The Yaam Club beach on the Spree River, near Oberbaumbrücke
(photo: Mathias Schormann © 1997)

The Field of Temporary Structures

Benjamin Foerster-Baldenius

Summer ´96

After five years of self-organized renovation on our house, the twenty-by-twenty meter open space in the front was transformed into our concrete production site. Officially the space is designated to become a "pocket park," which we decide to use for experimental public projects. We see a chance to redefine the terms "park" and "public space."

Winter ´96/97

We organize a competition, offering as first prize a full-service weekend in our Masonite luxury suite with balcony and view of the construction site. The jury decides on a proposal by Christoph Brucker: a forest of one hundred five-meter-high metal poles standing upright in the concrete that covers the whole space.

Spring ´97

We find sponsorship to drill the one hundred holes and a scaffolding company that will lend us their material. We get one thousand euros from the local cultural office to support a program in the summer. We then founded an Institute of Applied Building Arts, to invent constantly changing installations. We manage to involve several of the competitors to use the forest structure to realize their ideas.

Summer ´97

Every Sunday we surprise the neighborhood with exchange markets, clothing give-aways, a labyrinth, theater performances, concerts, kitchens, bars, light shows, an urban playground. Although the space is open to the street and the program is very public, most of the neighbors stay outside and watch from a distance.

Winter ´97/98

While we install the high-rise forest with old Christmas trees, we work on the next year's public projects. Following a suggestion of an honorable member of the Institute, Tadashi Kawamata, we separate the Institute from the site, by creating the Symposium for Contemporary Actionism.

Spring ´98

Ines Schaber calls me up. She's looking for a place to put up a *raumerweiterungshalle* (space-extending hall). She wants to pick it up from a German Democratic Republic summer camp at the Baltic Sea. The building, which we call the Pleasuredome, is a unique invention of GDR architects: an extendable container in astonishing ´70s design.

Summer ´98

The Pleasuredome houses numerous events, exhibitions, bars, concerts, movies, festivals, and ice cream shops . . . inside and somehow less public.

The sociologist Peter Arlt contacts me to propose a public bath for next year. To me it seems too risky and expensive. So we develop a new idea for a container hotel, and try to get funding, but fail. We return to the public bath idea. For the project *Bad ly*, we build pools out of (new) garbage containers, a beach (the first of many urban beaches), a kiosk, a dance floor, and a fence. *Bad ly* becomes our most successful project for attracting public participation: lots of neighbors use our private land. The people (and media) of Berlin like to look and go behind fences.

Winter ´98/99

I have to admit that with all these activities we have motored the gentrification process in our urban surroundings. People like to live where the artists are. As soon as we noticed that, we stopped our activity and started working on projects less close to our home to use the gentrification strategy in places that really need it like Halle Neustadt.

1 *Bad ly*, the smallest public bath in Berlin (photo: Martin Kaltwasser © 1997)

2 *Houses without Shadow*, a temporary labyrinth. Berlin (photo: Matthias Rick © 1997)The foundation of The

3 Institute of Applied Building Art. Berlin (photo: Matthias Rick © 1997)

4 The High-rise Christmas Forest. Berlin (photo: Matthias Rick © 1998)

5 The uplifted Space Extension Hall in the backyard. Berlin (photo: Matthias Rick © 1998)

6 *Immobil*, a festival around a caravan in the Space Extension Hall. Berlin (photo: Matthias Rick © 1997)

7 *Bad ly*, family fun in the water cascades. Berlin (photo: Martin Kaltwasser © 1997)

BAR / GDR / FRG
(BRQ / DDR / BRD)

Four-channel video, 36.01 minutes
Metro Detroit (2004)

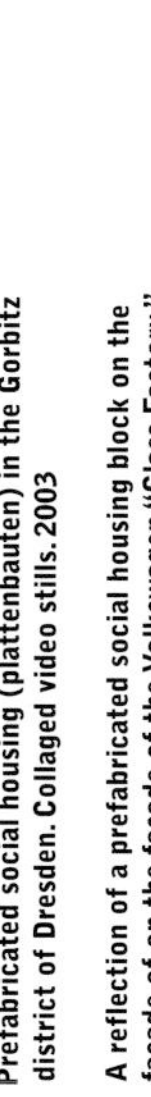

1 Prefabricated social housing (plattenbauten) in the Gorbitz district of Dresden. Collaged video stills. 2003

2 A reflection of a prefabricated social housing block on the façade of on the facade of the Volkswagen "Glass Factory." Collaged video stills. 2003

After its historical center was firebombed in 1945, Dresden has been boldly reconstructing itself. But the city has had difficulty choosing a single identity, vacillating between modernist forms that refute its aristocratic past, and the current westernization that is both nostalgic and bourgeois. Meanwhile, the restoration of its Baroque heritage continues. Thus Dresden now has three cities—each with its own physical ideology—battling for spatial dominance within the city center. Through processes of covering, removing, blocking, and enclosing, and changing colors, surfaces, and patterns, the war continues in Dresden, this time in peace, but still through architecture.

I have seen . . . I have seen . . . I have seen . . . the reconstruction of the Frauenkirche [church of our holy woman], like my plan from 1946 already shows.

If I am allowed to talk . . . If I am allowed to talk . . . I have seen . . . the liquidation of the Altmarkt [old market]; yes, the liquidation of the Altmarkt . . . I have seen . . . I have seen . . . Semperoper, Japanisches Palais, Blockhaus in the Neustadt, Neustädter Markt . . . were liquidated, a complete ruin of the town.

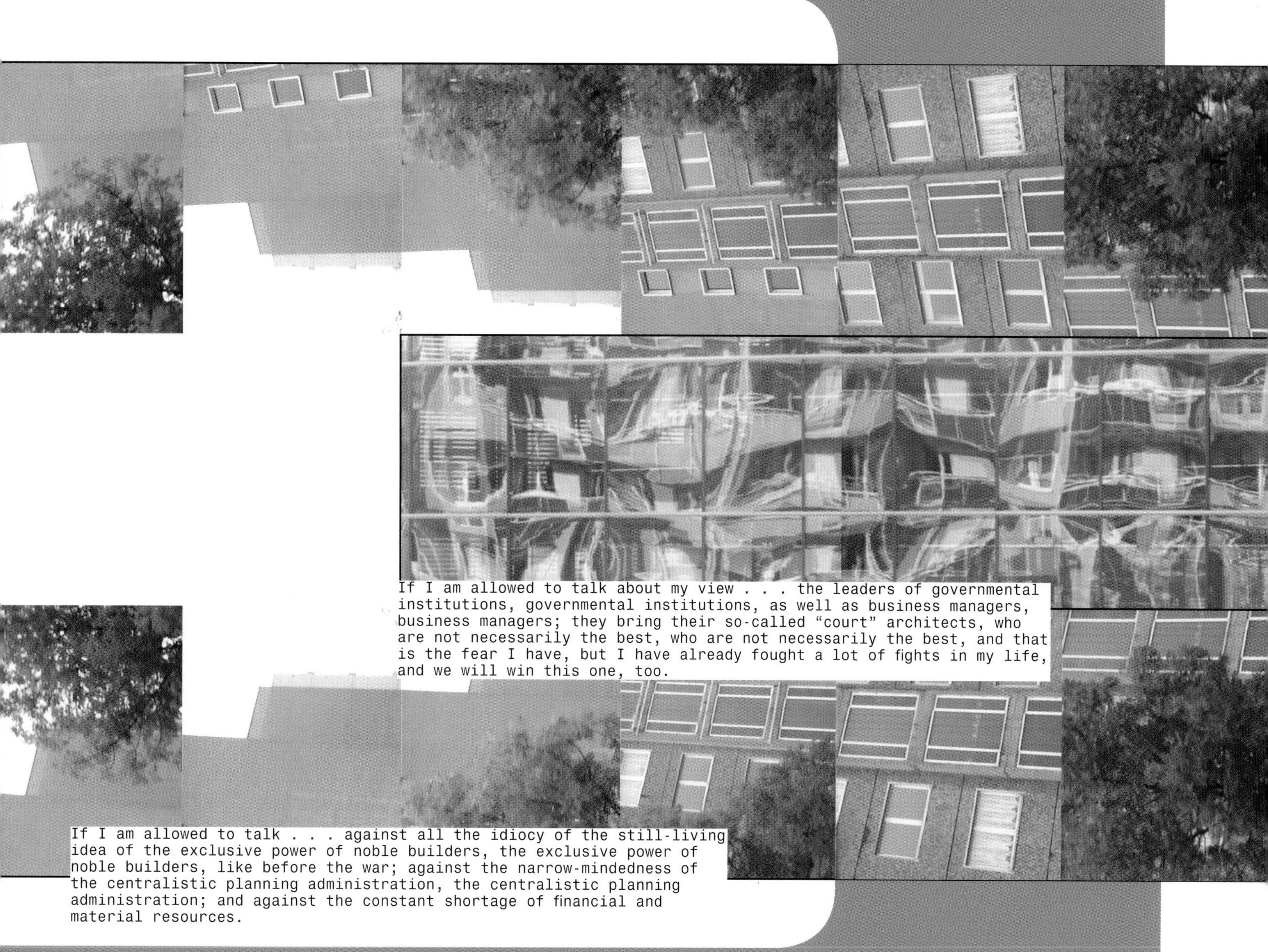

If I am allowed to talk about my view . . . the leaders of governmental institutions, governmental institutions, as well as business managers, business managers; they bring their so-called “court” architects, who are not necessarily the best, who are not necessarily the best, and that is the fear I have, but I have already fought a lot of fights in my life, and we will win this one, too.

If I am allowed to talk . . . against all the idiocy of the still-living idea of the exclusive power of noble builders, the exclusive power of noble builders, like before the war; against the narrow-mindedness of the centralistic planning administration, the centralistic planning administration; and against the constant shortage of financial and material resources.

I have seen . . . banks, and banks, and construction sites for future banks, banks.

At that point I said to Walter Ulbricht [one of the leaders of the former German Democratic Republic] . . . as long . . . as long as I live . . . as long as I live there . . . as long as I live there won't be a skyscraper in Dresden . . . and that is documented . . . and for that I was dismissed within the next three days . . . three days.

Of these five exciting years after the wall came down . . . it is astonishing how easy people have decided for demolition, for demolition, demolition [years ago since unification].

Of these five exciting years after the wall came down . . . [and then] they passively have to watch how urbane star architects or cool old hands quickly reduce or enlarge a market place, make abstract lines over hidden ground plans or create other facts, other facts, facts.

I have seen . . . villas, residences, and other condominiums with low tax liability, all of them for expensive tastes, tastes.

I have seen . . . car dealers, and savings banks, and office buildings,

and business centers, located in the best areas of town, equipped as modernly as possible, the best areas of town.

I have seen . . . business parks, residential parks, and fun parks;

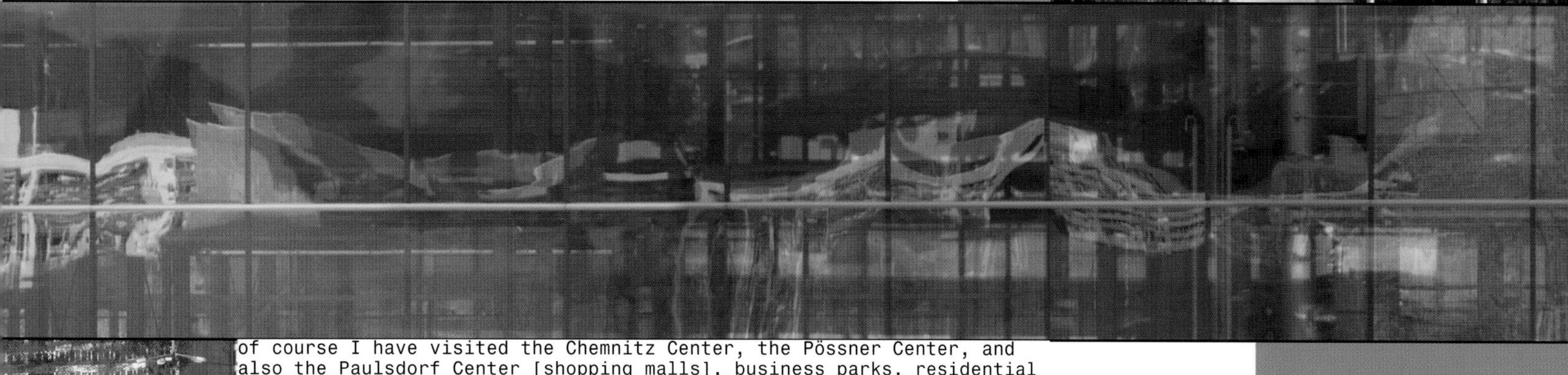

of course I have visited the Chemnitz Center, the Pössner Center, and also the Paulsdorf Center [shopping malls], business parks, residential parks, and fun parks.

I have seen . . . a giant building boom, a giant building boom, which, as soon as the long awaited revival takes command, living conditions are

4

turned inside out, completely changing the familiar environment until it is unrecognizable, unrecognizable; that, by the way, fundamentally distinguishes this building boom from the reconstruction work after the Second World War in both parts of Germany and also from the undesirable conditions in the GDR, where we were left out of planning, left out of planning and deciding too; but the ones who planned and built then were also prisoners of the system, prisoners of the system, like everybody else, like everybody else.

The question is . . . the question is . . . what holds the city together . . . together . . . together . . . we don't know . . . we don't know at all . . . how the people . . . we don't know at all . . . how the people behave and it would be a big mistake if we believed that we,

as architects or politicians or as the church, could give the people precise projections and expect them to conform to that.

It is a question . . . it is a question . . . that has to be asked for the entire society, too. There is no reason to resist investment pressure; but we

have to find the right way to handle this pressure. On the other hand, Dresden has a huge opportunity to set up a positive urban development and to realize it within the coming years, and the public of Dresden is one of the most important partners for the development of Dresden as a City of Art and Culture.

We . . . lack the desire . . . lack the desire of expressing . . . the time . . . the time that we live in . . . to demolish . . . to demolish . . . giant building boom . . . giant building boom . . . to demolish giant building boom . . . to demolish giant building boom.

Culture alone won't achieve it . . . alone won't achieve it . . . to demolish . . . to demolish . . . giant building boom . . . giant building boom . . . to demolish giant building boom . . . to demolish giant building boom.

Today the most important question is who owns the land . . . the land . . . to demolish . . . to demolish . . . giant building boom . . . giant building boom . . . to demolish giant building boom . . . to demolish giant building boom.

I assume that the decay can be halted . . . at the Elbe . . . now we must see that we don't cement anything that still needs to be changed

And this is really unique in Europe and needs to be preserved . . . in two or three years we'll demolish it again, won't we? . . . in two or three years we'll demolish it again, won't we?

Dresden has a huge opportunity . . . to set up a positive urban development
Dresden has a huge opportunity . . . the development of Dresden as a City of Art and Culture
Dresden has a huge opportunity . . . to demolish it, to demolish it, to demolish it, to demolish it

Today the most important question is who owns the land . . . the land . . . If I am allowed to talk about my view . . . If I am allowed to talk.

3 The new Volkswagen assembly plant, known as the "Glass Factory." 2003

4 Plauttenbauten on Winterberg Str. and Zwlingli Str., directly across from the Volkswagen "Glass Factory." Demolition of these plattenbauten has begun. 2003

5 Zwinger Royal Palace, together with Semperoper (Semper Opera House), the Hofkirche (Cathedral), FrauenKirche (Women's Church), and the Academy of Arts and Art Society forms an impressive Baroque architectural ensemble along Brühl's Terraces that is known as the Canaletto View of the "Florence of the Elbe." 2003

6 A meeting of citizens and city officials on the future of Prager Str., which was considered to be the most complete socialist urban planning center during the German Democratic Republic period. Participants were trying to find a negotiated solution to the disappearance of socialist architecture and commercialization of its public spaces. The meeting took place at a former community center, above a hi-rise hotel on Prager Str. 2003

7 BAR/GDR/FRG projected inside the construction site of the unfinished Wiener Platz development could be viewed from the pedestrian bridge that connected Hauptbahnhof (the main train station) and Prager Str. 2003

There Is Absolutely Nothing Left for You to Do

Christoph Schäfer

Around me, houses were waiting. It was a day in 1986, during the longest Sunday the world had ever seen, a Sunday that had begun eighteen years before. The city was under control, and worse, it was finished, completed. No one read Marcuse anymore and no one took him seriously either. Everything seemed predictable, like a remote-controlled dream walk. Worse even: the songs describing this state of mind had been written, had been sung. And still, nothing changed. Streets were lined by the number of trees and playgrounds prescribed by law, and people were walking their dogs between calm, working-class brick houses and nineteenth-century buildings freshly renovated in washable paint. On every second corner a planter with shrubs was placed, but no one could say who had placed it there, or why.

Alienation is a bad concept, I had learned from someone who had read a book I hadn't. But how about this type of alienation, of a life lived in a welfare cotton wool state. The whole city was saying: there is absolutely nothing left for you to do.

Have you ever had this thought? I thought it on a walk that day, down a street in Hamburg Barmbek. The wind was gripping my hair; it was April, sunny but cold, and the winter had not completely left town yet, when my eye caught hold of a new label in a new shop selling skateboards and skateboard fashion. It was the point, I would figure later, when skateboarding had radicalized, and teamed up with punk. The phrase on that label would change my thinking forever.
It said:

LIFE'S A BEACH

I take for granted you understand the wordplay. I didn't. I took it literally, and that set me thinking.

In the late `60s, the anti-alienation forces from Frankfurt's New Left said: *Under the pavement is the beach.* This sentence built a binary opposition between the alienated life represented by the pavement, and the supposedly unalienated life one would lead after the pavement had been removed; in other words, after the revolution, or in nature. The wittiness of the skateboarding

Filiz and her cousin Polly on the Palm Tree Island in the park, Hamburg. (photo: Margit Czenki © 2003, Park Fiction Archive)

sentence, however, reveals a lot about the social ramifications of this practice. Skateboarding only becomes possible in a situation, alienated as described above, full of concrete, sealed surfaces, asphalt, and skateable abstract art in public spaces. All the facilities placed in public space by an anonymous hand—the handrails, the concrete flowerpots, the pedestrian zones, the parking lots—are not the obstacle, but the precondition for skateboarding, a practice that, by misusing these facilities, redefines them at the same time.

The sentence thus marks a shift of paradigm, and suggests that good art, like the skateboard, has to work as a device that allows you to see the world in a different way and make new uses of it. A platform on wheels.

When I joined the Park Fiction group some years later, the basic confrontation could still have been understood along the lines of the pavement versus the beach. The city wanted to block the last view over the harbor with an expensive row of houses, whereas we, in the neighborhood, wanted a public park instead. Privatized view versus socialized shadow. But we refused to think along cherished lines of activism and developed a different way of operating. We avoided adressing the state in the language of protest and demonstrations. In our local, unrevolutionary situation, we started a parallel planning process in the community, and opened up the disputed field for a collective production of desires. This process was of course much more fun, and it also allowed for more complex ways of thinking and presenting. We could offer a vision, a platform for discussion and exchange of ideas, whereas traditional resistance groups focused on the state, and were reduced to saying "no" to the "visions" of investors. We turned the situation around; we quoted and played with the visionary vocabulary of image-city strategists, and suddenly it was the politicians who looked like uninspired and boring naysayers.

Years have gone by, and finally, in 2003, the first part of the desired park has been realised. It has taken too long, and some ideas have been damaged on the way by the bureaucratic process. However, the project was successful because neighbors and people from the subcultures joined forces; a struggle for a justified social cause and a politics of desiring teamed up during a time of boring authoritarian urban planning. This era is now in decline, and strangely, the project becomes real as the nation-state retreats from public responsibilities.

Shortly before we started, the Zapatistas said they had decided to stop preaching to people and to start listening. As much as this shift marks a dramatic rupture in revolutionary thinking and practice, today's projects that manage to build platforms of cooperation and link the everyday with the imaginary mark a change for art, social practices, architecture, and urban planning. At a time when the crisis in Argentina looks like the model of a situation that will reach the centers of capital sooner or later, small initiatives like the Park Fiction project are letters from an about-to-vanish-past to a very near future, when we will have to reinvent cities and everyday life on a much bigger scale.

Resident with desire for park, during Park Fiction 3, Hamburg, 1995. The Board says: Hedge cut in the shape of a poodle. (photo: Sven Barske © 1995, Park Fiction Archive)

Belgrade is a city that has been liberated many times, most recently on October 20th 1944, when Tito's partisans seized the city from the German occupiers. Liberating the streets of Belgrade led to the practice of discharging old, and loading new meanings that continues today. However, residue from the discharge of the previous systems lingers and still remains visible around the city as leaderships come and go, only partially installing their rhetoric. This accumulation of commingled dust and dirt obscures attempts to pin down or return to a specific identity.

The process of liberation does not only consist of removing an oppressive power but also of internalizing this situation and forging one's own identity in a changed environment. Many Jews in Serbia had to change their names to avoid deportation and murderous violence. This presents a strange instance of freedom to construct a new persona, an opportunity for choice that does not usually exist. For some, this change of names became an alluring new start, but for Moritz Levi, it was simply a temporary "freedom" that lasted only for the five years of liberation. He chose the purified Christian imagery of the angel for both his new first and last names: Andjelko Andjelkovic. He could not have sounded more innocent to his potential murderers. This strategy of survival shifted with the liberation from the German occupation, and he exchanged his personal renaming—a freedom born of necessity—for political liberation.

The alteration of names to indicate belonging, as well as the reappropriation of names after the liberation applies to streets and buildings as well as to individuals. After October 20th 1944 hundreds of streets that had been named for Serbian kings were renamed for communist partisan liberators and ideas of revolution. This process of renaming has become very accepted over the decades and has even gathered speed so that with each change the citizens and powers already anticipate the next change to come in the future. The names of streets, analogous to the temporary nature of politicians' careers in the city, are seen as fleeting, and changes are not always carried through fully; street plaques that should replace each other instead act like compounds. For instance, the name of Marshal Tolbuhin (a World War II general who died in a plane crash near Belgrade while coming to celebrate the twentieth anniversary of the October 20th liberation) was dubbed over the name MacKenzie (a Scottish World War I general) to create something like a fictional Marshezie's Street. In quickly animated Cyrillic, letters of old and new street names merge to create a hybrid set of names and meanings leading to a new fictitious map of the city.

Housing block number 23 was built mainly for the liberators of Belgrade during World War II. Today, twenty-seven liberators live in this building. New Belgrade, Serbia (photo: Jelena Mitrovic © 2003)

Looking for October
Contemporary Meanings of Liberation

Srdjan Jovanovic Weiss & Katherine Carl

This keeps the streets liberated from repeated renaming and lets everyone give their own names to the streets.

Similar alterations also take place also in the identity of buildings. October the 20th Elementary School located in the 70th housing block in New Belgrade was built in the '70s as exemplary brutalist architecture. Today, with the demise of liberal communism, it is a place of metamorphosis as the Orthodox Church regains status. A fresco of five Belgrade liberators of different eras from 1806, 1815, 1867, 1918, and 1944, is now accompanied by a bright mosaic of the patron saint of Serbia, Saint Sava. As one student put it, the saint is revered because he "helped many people by building schools." It seems only a matter of time until the brutalist building is renamed for the saint. What will the new generations attending lessons there make of this layering?

The replacement of the name of the Luxor Cinema in 1944 with the name October 20th points to popular culture's role in building history. A series of yearly cross sections of the building presents a dynamic pulsation of usage through time: the evolution of the content of movies shown there (from Russian partisan to Bruce Lee to Hollywood), and the numerous socialist youth organizations (from folklore dance to journalist clubs) that once used the space to upload partisan culture into the youth. Today it is simply a movie theater that screened the film *Tomb Raider*, the story of a government operative liberating treasures of the dead city, on October 20th 2003.

Another shift has occurred over the fifty years of liberation in the holiday's representation in the media. The main daily paper *Politika* does not follow a standard for promoting the liberation day of Belgrade. What one would expect to be a monumental date commemorated each year on the front page is instead mentioned inconsistently: some years covered in a full page, but often mixed with completely unrelated news and advertising. In contrast to Stalin's fixation on memorial propaganda backed up by violence, this randomization of memory is an indication that Belgrade feels that it does not need to remind the country of its partisan origins. When the October 20th holiday was no longer celebrated in 2003, there was no reaction in the media.

How will the future unfold for a city that can absorb so many self-made identities and that can hold together so many different—even opposing and unfinished—historical versions of itself?

View of housing block number 23 towards the "West Gate" of New Belgrade. New Belgrade, a city for 220,000 inhabitants, was built as an immediate follow-up to the liberation of Belgrade during World War II. (photo: Jelena Mitrovic © 2003)

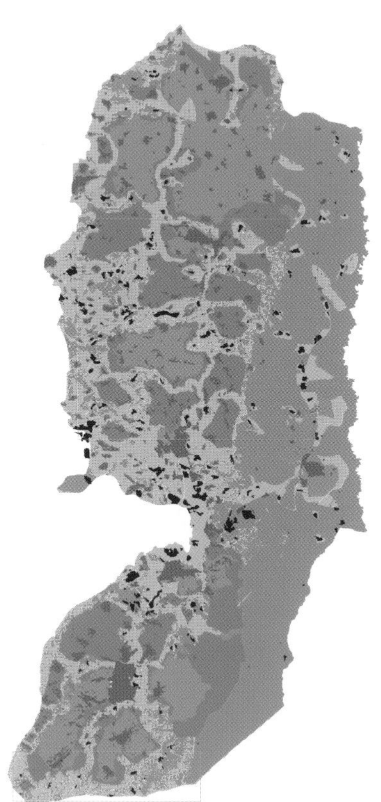

Settlement patterns of Isrealis and Palestanians in the West Bank. (photo: Eyal Weizmann © 2002)

Since the 1967 war, when Israel occupied the West Bank and the Gaza strip, a colossal project of strategic, territorial, and architectural planning has been at the heart of the Israeli-Palestinian conflict.

The landscape and the built environment became the arena of conflict. Jewish settlements—state-sponsored islands of territorial and personal democracy, manifestations of the Zionist pioneering ethos—were placed on hilltops overlooking the dense and rapidly changing fabric of the Palestinian cities and villages. First and third worlds spread out in a fragmented patchwork: a territorial ecosystem of externally alienated, internally homogenized enclaves located next to, within, above, or below each other. The border ceased to be a single continuous line and was broken up into a series of separate makeshift boundaries, internal checkpoints, and security apparatuses.

The total fragmentation of the terrain on plan demanded a design of continuity across the territorial section. Israeli roads and infrastructure thereafter connected settlements while spanning over Palestinian lands or diving underneath them. Along these same lines, Ariel Sharon's most recent plan proposes a Palestinian State on a few estranged territorial enclaves connected by tunnels and bridges, while further insisting that Israel would retain sovereignty over the water aquifers underneath Palestinian areas and the airspace and electromagnetic fields above them. Indeed, a new way of imagining territory was developed for the West Bank. The region was no longer seen as a two-dimensional surface of a single territory, but as a large three-dimensional volume, containing a layered series of ethnic, political and strategic territories. Separate security corridors, infrastructure, and underground resources were thus woven into an Escher-like space that struggled to multiply a single territorial reality.

What was often described by the historian Meron Benvenisti as crashing "three-dimensional space into six dimensions—three Jewish and three Arab" became the complete physical partitioning of the West Bank into two separate but overlapping national geographies in volume across territorial cross sections, rather than on a planar surface.

The process that split a single territory into a series of territories is a *politics of verticality.*

The Politics of Verticality

Eyal Weizman

Eyal Weizman, **TUNNEL ROADS**, a collage of the wall according to expropriation orders, 2004 (photo: Daniel Bauer © 2002)

Beginning as a set of ideas, policies, projects, and regulations proposed by Israeli state-technocrats, generals, archaeologists, planners, and road engineers since the beginning of the occupation of the West Bank, it has by now become the common practice of exercising territorial control as well as the dimension within which territorial solutions are sought.

Settlement master planners like Matityahu Drobles and Ariel Sharon aimed to generate territorial control from high points. Former U.S. president Bill Clinton sincerely believed in a vertical solution to the problem of partitioning the Temple Mount where Palestinians would own the mosques and the square in front of them while Israel would own the ground under and the air over them. Ron Pundak, the architect of the Oslo Accords, described solutions for partitioning the West Bank with a three-dimensional matrix of roads and tunnels as the only practical way to divide an undividable territory. And Gilead Sher, Israeli chief negotiator at Camp David (and a divorce lawyer), explained it to me as a simple negotiation and bridging technique—an apparent enlarging of the "cake" to be partitioned so that each side feels it is getting more.

OldHouseNewHouse/ NewCityOldCity

Four-channel video, 36.01 minutes
Metro Detroit (2004)

OldHouseNewHouse/NewCityOldCity is a project that inspects why some individuals and families have moved out of Detroit, or were unable to move, from one house to another, one hood to another, one city to another. Starting from the most recent house, and tracing each subject back to previous houses, the video follows the work and life of individuals and families, and also their memories and thoughts about the future. Comparing the decline of Detroit and the growth of its suburbs, **OldHouseNewHouse/NewCityOldCity** creates a physical and historical record of capital, labor, and cities that are becoming more nomadic than ever in the postmodern cultures of the developed nations.

Virginia
The hub of this community was the elementary school. We had two large churches here. All kinds of restaurants. And we had five movie houses. People could stay right here because we had everything.

Charles' friend
We had a Laundromat out there, a Coney Island joint. The restaurant, the shoeshine, the hat cleaning place, the hardware [store] that was up there. All you had to walk off three, four blocks and you could get anything you wanted.

Virginia
The population at that time, in this neighborhood, was probably four thousand or more families, and there was a house on every single lot.

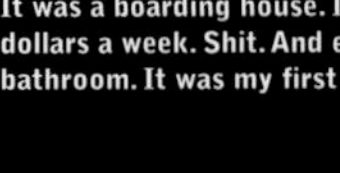

Charles
It was a boarding house. I paid twenty-five dollars a week. Shit. And everybody shared one bathroom. It was my first house.

Virginia
Right now, there are seven families left in the eighty-three acres [here].

Charles
So, in 1997 [city officials] said, "This is going to be a redevelopment area, and you are not going to be part of this. . . . If you don't sell us your house then we will declare eminent domain, and we will take your house." So that was the beginning of the end of this neighborhood.

Virginia
The city council had voted to take this [land] and declare eminent domain, and that was it.

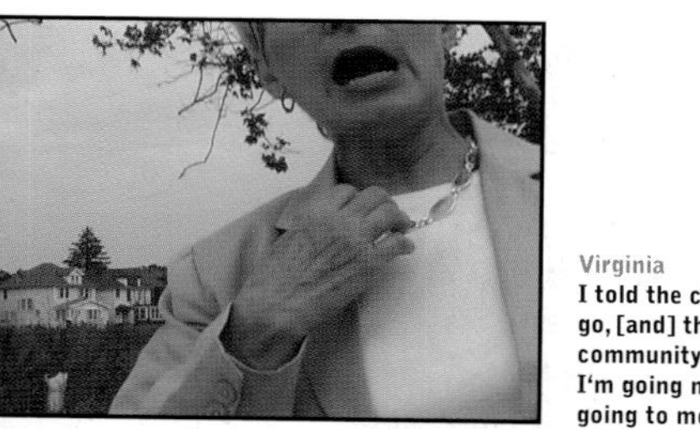

Virginia
I told the city at the meeting that I will not go, [and] that is my home, [and] this is my community. I've been here for forty-six years; I'm going nowhere. And the only time I'm going to move is when I decide to move.

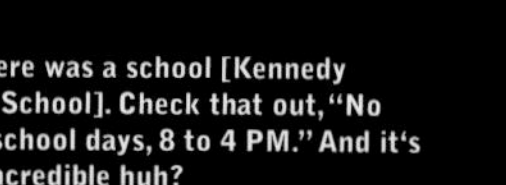

Charles
This right here was a school [Kennedy Elementary School]. Check that out, "No parking on school days, 8 to 4 PM." And it's still there, incredible huh?

Charles
This is where I lived with my mama and daddy before they divorced, right here. That's where the house was.

Charles
That ain't what we've got now. That's a lot of [empty] land here, ain't it?

Charles
We are the richest country in the world right? We should have health care, automatic, by law, [and] free! [A] motherfucker gets sick, [then] go to the motherfucking doctor! And none of us should pay for that shit.

Virginia
The day they came to tear down the church, my husband and me asked them if they could please leave those trees. [But] they cut this big huge tree down [that] was 137 years old. You destroy the whole community, [and] you destroy people's homes, but the least you could do is leave the tree that's been here for one hundred plus years.

Charles
There was a store on that corner right there. Ain't that something? The phone [booth] is [still] there but the building is gone. Ain't that something?

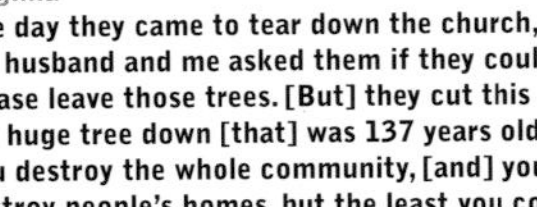

Virginia
This is my home, and I intend to stay in this home until I get ready to go to my final home. And that's going to be of my choosing and the Lord's choosing, not the city.

Charles
I know all the people in the neighborhood, they [all] know me.
Jane
I could count on the neighbors, and they were more willing to help than [my] family was.

Mario
I feel very much at home, I feel very safe here.
John
Safety, quality of life here.
Scott
[In] this community we watch out for each other.

Scott
Better suited for our lifestyle and has everything we could possibly want in a home.
Audra
It's an American dream, to have a good life and have money.

Mario
Everybody's lawn was manicured, there was pride in their property.
Randy
A great neighborhood, I'm telling you, like one in a million.

John
People wanted lower taxes, [and] wanted more space.
Michelle
A dream home . . . a house that is perfect, [and] that has everything you want in it.

Mario
Back on those days when they built a home, they built a home. It was solid.
Cassandra
The houses were kept up, and there weren't any empty or vacant spaces like it is now.

Michelle
It has every single store or restaurant you could ever possibly need, within a mile from my house. Everything is new, the house is new, schools are new, [and] that's what I like about it.

Randy
The riots killed downtown. Was I scared out of my mind. I saw the burning buildings.
Mario
Well my folks left [Detroit] right after the riot.

Michelle
We moved out here and paid $50,000 less for this house. It's brand new and so much bigger. And we will make $80,000 dollars when we sell this house.

Mario
All the burnt houses, and all the properties and buildings that are just abandoned. Thousands of them.
John
We had to remove lots of the structures that were not cost effective to restore.

Charles
They had dope going all up and down the street.
Lorenzo
It [was] scary to be outside, and it was not a safe place to live.

Scott
Walking, on the sidewalks, [or] down the side of the streets. Not everybody has a car down there [in Detroit]. In the city you walk.

Randy
Urban pioneers. I want to be one of those guys that move back into the city, to an old house, and fix it. You know those old beautiful houses.
Audra
Families living together, [and] helping each other out.

Scott
A great community, at a great price. And they are developing three or four miles beyond [here], and continuously going where the land is cheaper.

Toni
There's not that many places to go [here], like there's no museums.
Cassandra
Ah, recreation. We just drive around.

Cassandra
My kids don't have any friends on our block.
Rudy
In the suburbs everybody go behind their walls and that's it.
Jane
So isolated. I just felt like "Gosh, we are not part of the world anymore."

Michelle
Welcome! This is a three-bedroom, two full-bath Ranch. This is called the "great room" out here. We expanded it quite a bit from the original floor plan, so we bumped the kitchen out, [and] made it nice and big.

Michelle
He is so proud of his grass. It was all completely dirt when we bought this house. We had a sodding party one day and all of our friends and family came over, and we all threw the grass down.

Michelle
This is my daughter's bedroom. We love lavender. And purple is her favorite color, so everything is purple.

Ronnie
Over the years and months people kept setting [it] on fire. They were selling dope out of here, and then the police kept setting it on fire. But people still got to have somewhere to go. It's sad. But you got to do what you got to do, [and] come in here to sleep.

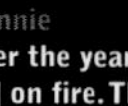

Ronnie
I stayed a winter and a summer here, but I had heaters. Yeah, I had propane heaters, had everything boarded up. I had plastic all over the windows to make sure everything was comfortable, so I wouldn't be too cold.

Ronnie
A guy died right in that bedroom. Right there. He caught on fire, [and] got burned up right in that room; an older guy.

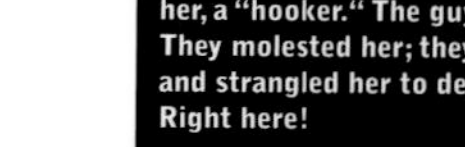

Ronnie
A girl got raped in this room and [they] killed her, a "hooker." The guys brought her up here. They molested her; they tied her arms together and strangled her to death right in this room. Right here!

Scott
None of this used to be here. Lot has changed. Lot of these subdivisions used to be golf courses.

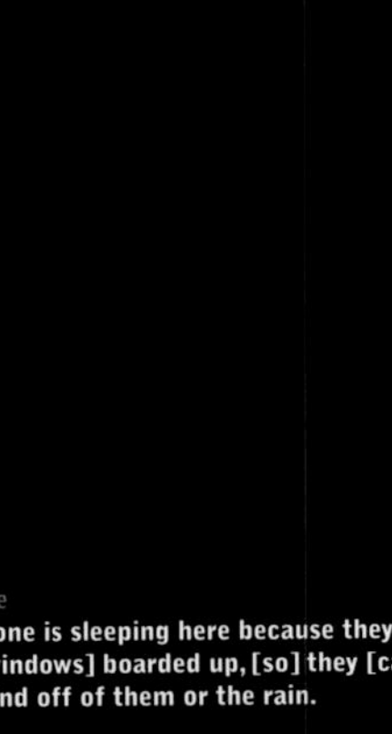

Ronnie
Someone is sleeping here because they got [the windows] boarded up, [so] they [can] keep the wind off of them or the rain.

Scott
Basically, in here, they have Ranches, which are one-level, [and] Colonials, which are two-levels, and the split levels, which is ours, a kind of a combination between a Ranch and a Colonial.

Ronnie
Like I said, over the years, of the fire damages [it] had, the building just started to come apart. And the way you keep taking [the] bricks away from it, you [are] taking support away from it.

Scott
They have different faces of the home called elevations you can choose. And each elevation costs, as you upgrade the elevation obviously the price [goes up].

Ronnie
You see people change their boots and stuff [here]. Hey, these are nice boots, man.

Scott
The master bath; this could be someone's apartment. There is one, two, three, four, five bathroom sinks [in the house].

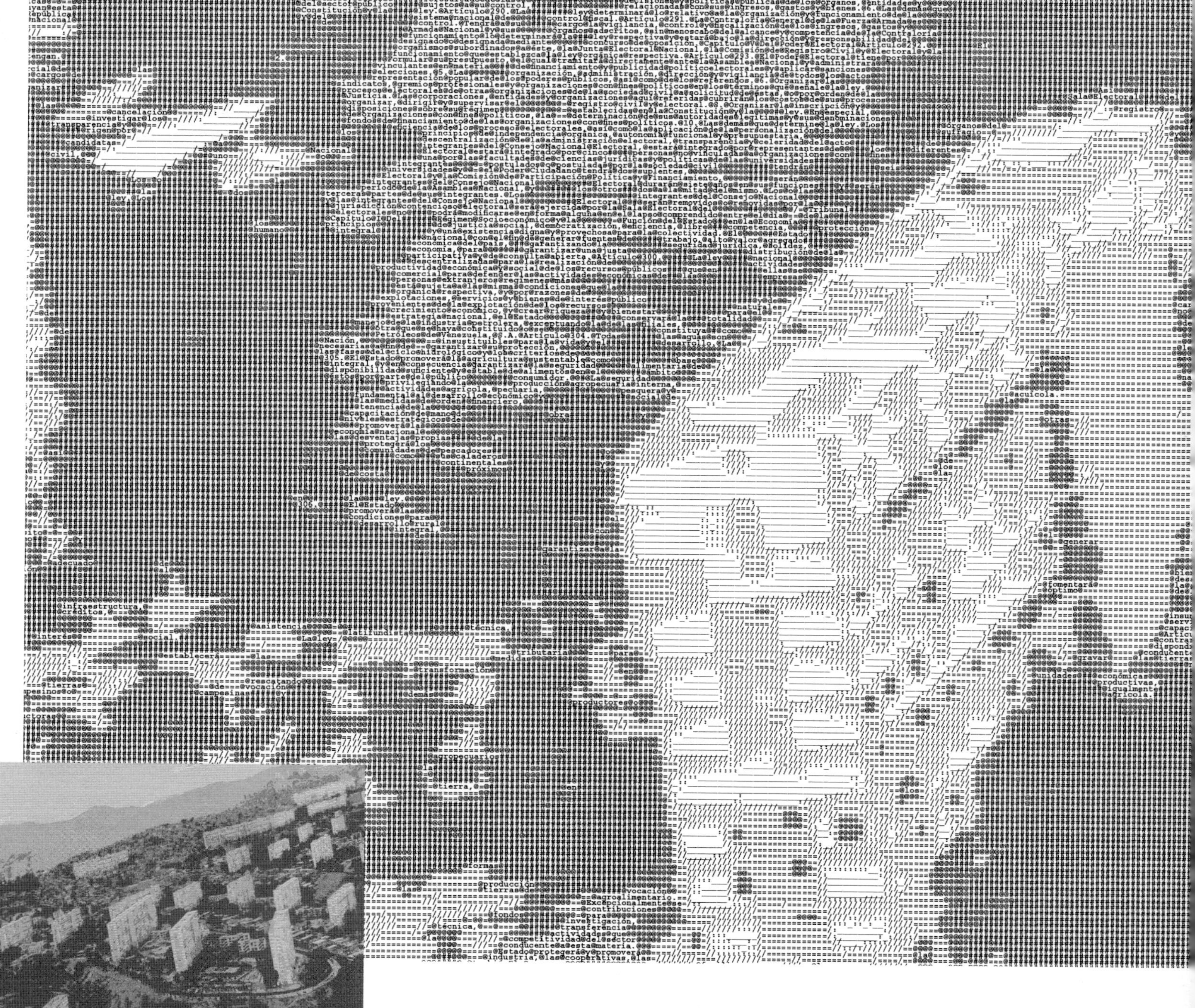

Aerial view of the modernist housing project 23 De Enero. Caracas (photo: Bitter/Weber © 2002)

The price is not more than twice the cost of an average European daily newspaper. We ask if we can get a better price if we buy three. They are small blue books, each slightly different. Some look generic, some very precious. Some of the mini-books say on the back: *constitution@yahoo.com*. They are popular knockoff versions of the Venezuelan state constitution which are sold in the street markets along with "Diezel-Jeans" and "adibas" t-shirts. We start to collect them.

The street life is busy, colorful, and noisy. Booths and tables of vendors create a thick layer of informal economy on the available public terrain between traffic and buildings. While the street markets seem prosperous, the architecture behind them appears rundown and abandoned, the residue of a past heyday of imported forms of modernization which failed to succeed. Caracas seems to be a city that is shrinking and expanding at the same time, struggling against corporate oligarchy and globalized neoliberal forces.

In Venezuela at this moment, participatory democracy is associated with the making of the new national constitution. It is one of the major projects of President Hugo Chavez Frias, who is leading the process of social, political, and economic transformation. When discussing the political and social transformation of Venezuela, it seems like everybody but the middle and upper classes carries the new constitution in their pocket. The neoliberal policies of the '90s left eighty percent of Venezuela's population in poverty; they have been engaged in making a new constitution and building a participatory democracy from the streets up.

Since the '60s, small self-organized groups of people, organizations, and communities have offered resistance to oppressive modernization and capitalism, and struggled for local power and a more just distribution of wealth. Their urban practices such as land reform committees or urban agriculture projects are related to programs and reforms administrated and executed from above by the new government, but forcefully initiated by the people from below. Inhabitants of the historic housing project 23 de Enero form one such community that seeks the transformation of a modernist rationality to an insurgent urbanism.

We meet organizers and members of the socially and culturally engaged community organization Coordinadora Simon Bolivar. Their office is located in a former butchershop, next to a grocery,

Let's Call it Participatory Modernism

Sabine Bitter & Helmut Weber

a coffee bar, and an electronics shop, all part of 23 de Enero. In only three years, from 1954-57, about nine thousand apartments were built in 23 de Enero under the dictatorship of Perez Jimenez.

Led by Venezuelan architect Carlos Raul Villanueva, the project of urbanization aimed to apply modernism to Venezuela and to eradicate the unsightly barrios from the surface of the city. Today people tell us that the superblocs are also called the vertical barrios.

Posters on the Coordinadora wall show Simon Bolivar, the liberator; another promotes the fight for local power; a third reports that there are many street children in the megacities of Latin America, but not one in Cuba. Are we back in the revolutionary '70s? As we drink Pepsi from plastic cups, we learn from the Coordinadora that during the uprising against the dictatorship in 1958, *campesinos* and the poor squatted in four thousand of the nine thousand apartments. Since the blocks were not finished, the people completed the buidling, putting in windows and doors individually. The façades still witness the process of appropriation of the modernist urban structures, but the alterations visually recall the participatory practices in architecture we know from the Netherlands or Belgium in the '70s.

We witness forms of urbanism in Caracas that are the engine of a greater social transformation. To represent that urbanism in our project *Caracas, hecho en Venezuela* (*Caracas, made in Venezuela*) and to link two productive processes occurring in Caracas—23 de Enero and the new Constitution—we altered an aerial image of 23 de Enero with software we developed. Through this process, the photograph is reconstructed with text characters of the entire 1999 Constitution of the Bolivarian Republic of Venezuela.

The fusion of megastructures—the new Constitution and 23 de Enero—speculates on possible forms of participatory modernism and relates collective practices which produce the new spatial relations of Caracas to Venezuelan participatory democracy. It points towards the necessity of scale jumping in current urban debates to articulate global forces in urban territories and local, community-based self-organizing practices to state responsibility.

What is happening in Paris' 13 arrondissement, where a high-rise residential building has been completely transformed by a population of Asian *émigrés*, who use the underground parking as a bazaar and the apartments as workshops?

Why does the center of San Marino, where nobody lives anymore, now function as a veritable shopping mall, with fixed opening hours?

And why has Elche, near Valencia, become a city completely dedicated to domestic labor, where thousands of apartments have machines for shoe manufacture in their kitchens?

Why is Switzerland, with the world's highest concentration of patents per capita, covered by hi-tech gardens where the most sophisticated innovations are developed?

How many know that two ethnic and religious communities have switched places across the sea between the Sicilian port Mazara del Vallo and the North African city of Tunis, reducing the distance between the two continents?

And what is happening in the Benelux[1], where frontiers between Belgium, Luxemburg, and the Netherlands attract a frenzied population of commuters that travel within a single, endless and generic city?

Why have the reclaimed Tyneside coal mines in England become a popular site for parachuting, clay-pigeon shooting, picnics, and other leisure activities?

How are we to decipher the paradox of Pristina, which, in spite of dramatic ethnic cleansing, has become Europe's most "mongrel" city, with more than sixty thousand foreigners from fifty countries including military forces and non-governmental organization members?

Why are public spaces and ground floors in Belgrade being invaded by a flood of commercial kiosques that has completely overtaken the existing shops and the street?

[1] A customs union comprising Belgium, the Netherlands, and Luxembourg.

And what is the map of the next rave parties, veritable erratic theme parks crossing Europe and gradually moving towards the east?

In a word, how is the European territory changing?
What drives these transformations?
And what is Europe today? Where does its territory end?

Almost seventy architects, researchers, photographers, filmmakers, artists, and geographers of the Multiplicity network have tried to answer these questions, identifying—as detectives of space—some of the processes that have been transforming the European territory and its cities, from Pristina to Paris, from Helsinki to Porto. These are unusual and little-known processes and phenomena, existing outside the current discourse on architecture and urbanism. Yet they wield great power, and are able to radically change the nature of the principal European cities.

The results of this survey form the ongoing research *USE–Uncertain States of Europe.*[2] *USE* uncovers the stories of these and other innovative sites throughout Europe. Instead of focusing on big architectural projects or public intervention plans, *USE* proposes an image of Europe as a cultural device always in movement that in these years is experiencing new self-organized aggregative forms and novel social landscapes. It is in these sites, at the periphery of its geopolitical imagery, that Europe is changing most rapidly. It is here that innovations emerge and it is possible to imagine the future of our continent.

2 *USE–Uncertain States of Europe* is a project by Multiplicity. It was shown in the exhibition *Mutations* (Bordeaux 2000, Tokyo 2001) and USE, *Dentro la Città Europa*, La Triennale di Milano (Milano 2003). *USE–Uncertain States of Europe* was published in *Mutations* (Actar: Barcelona, 2001, by various authors), *Mutations* (TN Probe: Tokyo, 2000, by various authors), and *USE–Uncertain States of Europe* (Skira: Milan, 2003, by Multiplicity).

Picturesque Industrialism, the Rouge Plant, Ford Motor Company, River Rouge just outside of Detroit (photo: Jerry Herron © 2004)

Not from Detroit

Jerry Herron

[1] "Detroit's Agony," *Prime Time Live*, ABC, 8 November 1990.

[2] See Witold Rybczynski, *City Life: Urban Expectations in a New World* (New York: Scribner, 1995), 175-76. See also Sam Roberts. *Who We Are: A Portrait of America* Based on the Latest U.S. Census (New York: Random House, 1993), 125-26.

[3] Quoted in Kenneth T. Jackson, *Crabgrass Frontier: The Suburbanization of the United States* (New York: Oxford Univ. Press, 1985), 175.

Here's the hidden-in-plain-sight secret that defines American character, and makes us the people we are. We are—all of us—not from Detroit. That's the one thing we all, indisputably, share: the insistent negative that drives us toward the fulfillment of our national ideal. Even people who actually are from Detroit—the 4.4 million citizens of the Primary Metropolitan Statistical Area, as the Census Bureau calls it—are, most of them, not from Detroit, where they never go, and where only 951,000 people still live. And even the people who live inside the old city limits, being good Americans, behave as if they don't live there either, at least not in the way we usually think of citizens inhabiting a city; as if they felt responsible for it, and for each other.

In that sense, Detroit is the most American site on the planet. Americans are post-historical individualists, always on the move. We want to live in bigger houses, on bigger lots, out in the country, away from town, with more cars in the garage than drivers. We never walk, we grow morbidly fat, we love our guns, and look upon violence as a constitutionally guaranteed right. We grow misty-eyed about freedom; meanwhile we lock up more of our own than any other country. "We're talking about Detroit," Diane Sawyer said, when *Prime Time Live* came to diagnose the city in 1990. "Once a symbol of U.S. competitive vitality, and some say still a symbol, a symbol of the future, the first urban domino to fall." [1]

That's the genius of TV journalists: they always know just where to look for symbols, but they never have a clue what they are seeing. Of course Detroit is poor and black and violent and empty. "Neighborhoods collapsed," former Mayor Coleman Young explained in the same *Prime Time* episode, "because half the goddam population left." Not by accident, of course, but by design, and that's the crucial point most people miss about Detroit, and about the unfolding of our national character.

Americans came late to cities; we didn't get to be an urban people until 1920. But we are quick studies. By 1970, the city was over as a destination; at least the old, central city was, where the majority no longer lived. We had moved on.[2] "The city is doomed," Henry Ford so providently, and profitably, observed. "We shall solve the city problem by leaving the city."[3]

So we drove away, as planned, on the freeway, leaving the past and all that goes with it in the rear-view mirror. Not because of either failure or fluke; however, but because of success, because the city taught us how to not need it any more, with Detroit being the most successfully superannuated city in this country, the place that more people are not from than any other.

Which leads to a great crisis of representation. If Detroit is no longer a city, then what is it? How do we talk about this past we prefer to be no longer from? How do we accept responsibility for the ignorant wasting on which our native prosperity depends? Yes, we are all not from Detroit: to our peril and humiliation, and perhaps doom.

A view of the downtown skyline, with the Renaissance Center being the biggest and tallest building. Nearby is the six-story-tall steel frame of an unfinished building. It was a private development that went wrong, a projected clubhouse and restaurant for a private yacht club. Its been empty for more than ten years. The city has an ample collection of failed resurrections, like this. The Renaissance Center, for instance, built in the early 1970s, at estimated today's cost of more than $2 billion, was the largest private urban development in American history. After failing to "renaissance" Detroit, which was its ideal, it was recently purchased by General Motors, to make its world headquarter for $75 million.

The power plant dominates the city of Ivanovo behind. A utopian image of a city powered by industrialism embraced the political contrarieties between the worlds of communism and capitalism. This image, with minor adaptations to local style and landscape around, could be found in other industrialized cities. In front was a pond where I saw three goats, many fishermen, and a young boy swimming while his mother watched.

Mariner's Wharf is a huge housing development on the waterfront south of Liverpool. Like the famous Albert Dock Village, it's an attempt to revive the city. Here is another generic and "gated community," conveniently exploiting the already segregated geography of a dock, to be away from the city and its many ailments.

CityMix

Four-channel video, 36.01 minutes
Metro Detroit, Halle/Leipzig, Ivanovo, Liverpool/Manchester (2004)

CityMix coalesces multiple urban landscapes, the four city-regions within the project *Shrinking Cities*—Detroit, Michigan; Halle/Leipzig, Germany; Ivanovo, Russia; and Liverpool/ Manchester, England—into synchronized panoramic views. Spaces and time, forms and sounds are blended together, creating landscapes of impressions that exist between the cities, not in each city.

While I was shooting at the outskirts of Sudstadt, a small *plattenbauten* city between Halle-Neustadt and the old Halle, hundreds of sheep came up the hill and surrounded me. Yes there was a modern day shepherd named Beund Wepnei who had plenty of open land for his flock to wander, between the new suburban villas and a regional Deutsche Telecom office building. Again it's a combination of what appeared since the unification, suburbanization with a future office park. At the distance are the infamous Silberhohe, one of the German Democratic Republic cities under a major demolition project now, and the smoke rising from the old state-owned Chemical Works Buna that once employed 30,000 workers in this chemical industry zone. The factory was the GDR's chemical industry zone, between the cities of Halle, Bitterfled, and Chemitz. Buna is now owned by Dow Chemicals and employees only few hundred workers; the efficiency of privatization. While I was shooting this panorama, a man with a briefcase walked by twice, following a foot trail into the woods. Was he late to Buna?

A view from a small old village at the edge of the Ivanovo city boundary, with the Sukhovka housing complex and a few other smaller satellite cities in the far distance, along with the cooling towers of power plant #3.

Norris Green in Liverpool was built in the 1930s. Now it's half demolished and is gradually being emptied out. Like in Detroit, it's amazing how people can maintain their homes and lives while their surroundings are empty and burning.

Just a few years old, The Great Indoors is the newest mall to join the four large shopping zones that are located around the clover- leafed ramps where Novi Road connects with interstate highway 69. With Novi Expo Center, Novi Town Center, and the Twelve Oaks Mall East and West, this intersection has supersized the traditional corner stores in cities. Together, the malls encompass one square mile, about the same area as downtown Detroit. It really is the new downtown for the city of Novi. The Great Indoors doesn't have the interior streets of a typical mall but instead, many stores are fed directly from a faux "cityscape" street.

A street in the Volksmarsdorf area of Leipzig, half empty and half renovated, although it seemed that most of the renovated flats were empty too. Leipzig, like most other cities in East Germany, is a mosaic of old and new, dark gray and light brown, faded and bright, demonstrating the invasion of the west and the disappearance of the east.

MODERN
SKATE & SURF
SALE
Straßen-
schäden
Einertstraße

RIZZO
Straßen-
schäde

Ancoats district in Manchester, a former industrial zone now turning commercial. The old canal is a new recreational pathway between new office buildings and an almost completely demolished council housing area where three of four tower blocks are empty.

The new "urban villas" contrast sharply with the older *plattenbauten* city in the Paunsdorf area at the outskirts of Leipzig. One is a city in a rural area, and the other is a rural area in a city. The idea of individualism and collectivism is very clear, but both deny the identity of the self within.

The Woodbridge Mansions recall Paunsdorf in Leipzig, but in three chapters: the downtown with its pre-depression skyscrapers from when Detroit was the wild city of industrial capitalism; the public housing project towers from its ideal city period; and now the New Urbanism in the suburbanization of city. It's a sequential time frame of a city that unfolds over space.

In Europe, Japan, and the United States the populations of cities are mostly stable or declining. The most serious problems there are not the ones caused by population explosions that are confronting cities in Asia, Latin America, and Africa. The challenge for the more stabilized countries is to find ways to use their wealth to achieve the promised ends of advanced industrial civilization: universal social justice, liberation from poverty and drudge labor, opportunities to learn and grow and be creative, and the chance to be fully realized individuals and not merely statistics, numbers, cogs in the machinery. Globalization, or what I call a trend toward monological thinking, exists only in terms of economic struggles for the worldwide hegemony of liberal capitalism. It keeps individuals submerged in a mass of consumers and works against many of these ends. So does demagogic political leadership, which maintains its power through the creation of fear, particularly of "others," who are portrayed as "hating our way of life." While people in the centers of global capital enjoy unprecedented benefits of human thought and invention, they live in an emotional atmosphere infected more and more by an almost medieval obsession with myths and magic, with fantasies of good and evil.

For the city in the most stable developed countries, the greatest challenge today is to create a ground for individual human beings that not only supports their legal, economic, and environmental rights, but also nurtures their sense of autonomy and personal responsibility toward others. The way to do this is to show people, by example, that their autonomy—their freedom—is dependent on the autonomy of others. That is a fact of the human condition. I cannot be free unless those I live with are also free.

There are many ways that architects can work to meet this challenge. The most obvious is to become aware of and to acknowledge in their practices the crises affecting the city they live in. This means not buying into the propaganda that the causes lie elsewhere, whether with the feared "others" or with uncomprehending and unresponsive clients. It means accepting personal and therefore professional responsibility for a particular state of affairs. It does not mean taking on every crisis or problem but addressing the ones an architect feels most capable of responding to creatively and effectively. Not every architect will want or be able to assume responsibility for problems outside the normal client-architect relationship, or for seeing the larger social issues within that relationship. This places a heavier burden of responsibility on those who do.

What is necessary here is a fundamental change in attitude. The architect who accepts responsibility is not someone who waits by the telephone for a client to call with a commission, but someone who is aware of the significant and complex role the design of space plays in realizing the social contract, and who by law is empowered to exercise authority over the process of design. This architect assumes a role of leadership in the design of space and takes the initiative. Clients have their vested interests, which include a very real social agency bestowed by virtue of the wealth and resources they control. But this does not supplant the agency of architects, which comes not from the control of society's wealth and resources, but from their stewardship of ideas and principles that govern how wealth and resources are to be used through the design of space.

Getting down to particulars, architects need to look critically at the whole question of building types. These types, which are the basis of architectural design, correspond to economic categories in the first place, but also to social stereotypes that organize the conventions governing social interactions. Apartment buildings, single-family houses, office buildings, shopping centers, hotels, memorials, parks, hospitals, theaters, and even streets and public spaces are the labels we put on our projects, and they relate almost mechanically to line items in accountants' ledgers: housing, clothing, food, entertainment, medical, transportation, leisure. That makes practical sense, and certainly organizes clients' programmatic directives to architects. The obvious problem with typing comes when we realize that the flow of urban living intermingles these categories, both socially and spatially, in ways that cannot, should not, be predictable or entirely controlled. Most people find ways around the rigidity of being office-like at the office, or home-like at home, so there is a lot of flexibility in the typological system that makes for a workable compromise between typing and flow. But typological thinking becomes a serious problem in critical or ambiguous situations, when some form of radical change is underway and the prevailing typologies are insufficient to accommodate them. Examples may range from war and natural disaster to economic collapse and reformation to the emergence of a long-repressed social group that upsets the existing order of beliefs. Types, or stereotypes, break down when confronted with change, because they cannot genuinely, or generously, embrace the new. This includes, ironically enough, types labeled "flexible," because they are commonly based on systems designed to accommodate only predicted changes.

If I could sketch out for architects a task list addressing the urgent problems of cities in the developed countries, it would certainly include—at the top of the list—the design of spaces serving human complexity and diversity in new ways. These spaces will not be characterized by ideas of indoor and outdoor, public and private, and a host of other commonly accepted distinctions. Instead, they will be conceived as elements in continually shifting urban fields that maintain a delicate balance between order and anarchy, between knowledge and the unknown, or perhaps, the unknowable. To design such spaces, architects will have to abandon stereotypes of the process as well as the product of design. Old ideas of the master architect, who holds tight control of the final product, will necessarily give way to the *magister ludi*, the master orchestrator of the game. The urban game, a very serious and consequential one that will involve many people with diverse interests, all of whom must find their place in the urban field, cannot be played with pre-determined goals and fixed rules. All is in flux. Yet this cannot mean anything goes, quite the contrary. Operating in the space between fixed order and unbridled chaos, the architect of the urban field works continually to design and revise the rules, and then lets others do the design of particular spaces. This will happen not only at the large scale of urban fabric, but in the design of individual buildings. The results will be the outcome of a complex collaboration, which we can only begin to visualize at present. Nevertheless, it is the task of architects who want to accept the challenge of the new demands of cities for spaces of complexity and diversity to begin this visualization process and to experiment in the formulation of new types of design processes and the rules governing them.

Hans Ulrich Obrist: You recently worked on a new urban project for New York. Five architects and urbanists were invited to rethink an area of the West Side of Manhattan.
Cedric Price: I wasn't the winner. I'm not surprised, because mine required commitment for a very long time. It was suggesting that this area of the West Side was the last vacant area allowing fresh air to come off the river, and therefore they should do very little with it; the last thing they should do was cover the railway and build over it. But all the other schemes did just that: they built a stadium, a thirty-thousand-seat center for something.

[HUO]: What role did the river play in your ideas?
CP: Well, the Hudson River is cleaning up all the time in any case. It's a fresh water river, and therefore I was aware of the vast amount of water running down the Hudson and into the ocean. And the winds are from the southwest and west, so the conditions were ideal without anything. The last thing I wanted to do was to increase the foul, static nature of the air by producing more buildings. New York suffers from over-development.

[HUO]: Can we talk about the city?
CP: A city that doesn't change and replace itself is a dead city, but the question is whether one should use the word "cities" anymore. I think it's a questionable term.

[HUO]: What could replace it?
CP: Certainly not "megalopolis" or anything like that, but it may be a word associated with the human awareness of time, turned into a noun which relates to space. I haven't thought of the word yet, but it shouldn't be too difficult. But the city changes all the time, so it cannot be a frozen word: it would have to be a word in permanent mutation. Cities exist for citizens, and if they don't work for citizens, they die. Only in over-educated, overpaid Western civilizations do people worry about dead cities—like Petra, or the biggest city in the world, Angkor Wat in Cambodia, which just vanished in the jungle because it wasn't needed any more.

[HUO]: So cities can die ...
CP: Oh yes. Cities die through lack of usefulness. Even something as vast as Angkor Wat lasted for less than two hundred years.

DEAD CITY

Hans Ulrich Obrist in conversation with Cedric Price

The former Michigan Central Railroad Station, Detroit. 2004

[HUO]: Let's talk about architecture ...

CP: I think that at the present architecture doesn't do enough. It doesn't enrich or enliven people's lives as much as, say, the Internet does, or a good story, or music. Architecture is a poor performer; it's consistently bad. As an architect, I'm trying to make architecture a better performer.

The history of Detroit has been inscribed by great arcs of production, economic downturns, and shifting populations. Its portrait has been shaped by cars, music, and media exposure that has perhaps relied more on caricature and negative representation than a more complex and truer presentation.

In 1999 I was invited by iCUE (International Center for Urban Ecology) to participate in a workshop focused on the near eastside of inner city Detroit. This area, demonized in recent times for the Devil's Night burnings, provided a contrary "green" inspiration to develop two new projects, S.P.O.R.E. (Sustainable Production Organized in Regard to the Environment) and S.P.A.W.N. (Specialized Project: Agriculture, Worms, Neighbors). Both of these projects were informed by an urban agrarian revolution that I found happening, yet tempered by the harsh reality of a community without the support of productive industry and still scarred by the rages and inequalities of the past.

The intention of these projects was to address the burned and abandoned houses, evidence of a destructive history standing block after block. By targeting the reconfiguration and potential reuse of the houses through the application of art and architecture practices, I saw a way to offer the neighborhood engaging, creative projects owned and propelled by the residents.

S.W.I.N.G. emerged from these earlier projects. The emphasis has shifted from individual projects to multiple sites throughout Detroit. Instead of only targeting blighted areas to "add culture," the task to artists and architects, both professionals and students, is to invent, with the people of the communities, projects to transform the disturbing destroyed-house icon into a new-use icon.

By removing a prejudice narrowly focused on art for "poor" neighborhoods, this approach encourages a creative challenge to residents, artists, and architects to ignore existing social/economic territories. S.W.I.N.G. will seek out abandoned property and houses with the goal of NOT rehabilitating or patching the condition, but of adding another evolution to a site through application of art and architectural imagination and innovative economic opportunity.

S.P.O.R.E. to S.W.I.N.G.

Mel Chin

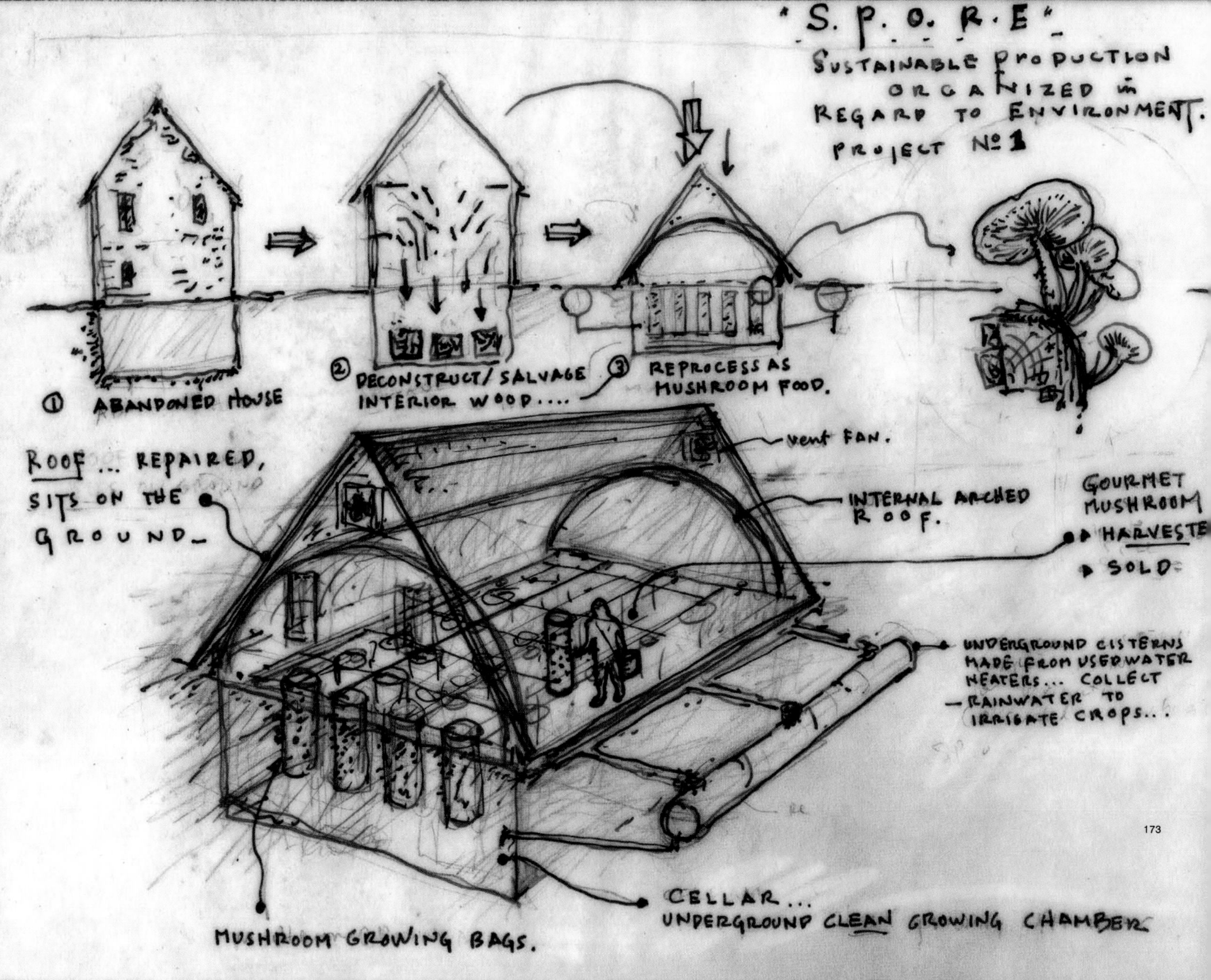
"S.P.O.R.E"
SUSTAINABLE PRODUCTION
ORGANIZED in
REGARD TO ENVIRONMENT.
PROJECT No 1
① ABANDONED HOUSE
② DECONSTRUCT/SALVAGE
INTERIOR WOOD....
③ REPROCESS AS
MUSHROOM FOOD.
ROOF... REPAIRED,
SITS ON THE
GROUND_
vent FAN.
INTERNAL ARCHED
ROOF.
GOURMET
MUSHROOM
▸ HARVESTE
▸ SOLD
UNDERGROUND CISTERNS
MADE FROM USED WATER
HEATERS... COLLECT
RAINWATER TO
IRRIGATE CROPS...
CELLAR...
UNDERGROUND CLEAN GROWING CHAMBER
MUSHROOM GROWING BAGS.

A sustainable premise is essential. The new projects must move away from the expected temporary art installation and housing rehabilitation. Instead, it must make a lasting contribution to the needs or the dreams of a specific neighborhood. The reconfigured house or lot will be used until it evolves into something else, useful to the community. S.W.I.N.G. is conceived as a flexible project that could support any number of creative adventures that serve the residents.

Imagine a small wooden structure in Chaldean Town that gives new meaning to the term "balloon framing." The walls, windows, and roof are blown into geometric bits, framed and captured in mid air, connected with steel frames and Thermopane—expanding the small cottage to become large enough to house a new community center.

Imagine a former house in the Five Points Community with only its roof remaining, inexplicably sitting on the ground. Concealed within are its salvaged wooden interiors, ground up, bagged, and hung in the basement as food for gourmet mushrooms (later food in fancy restaurants) in a state-of-the-art underground structure.

Come back to East Poletown to a house that pivots from a point on its foundation. Sunlight fills underground chambers revealing a worm farm. The worms composting the garden clippings and recycled newspapers are gathered to be sold to fisherman, and the worm castings are sold to local rose gardeners in Gross Pointe. The light necessary for the sorting process (separating worms from soil) makes the surreal action understood and pragmatic. It also reclaims the abandoned home from its negative association through function and enterprise.

S.W.I.N.G. will encourage neighborhood mixes where each community can show off its project and strategize on the co-evolution of their community with the artists and designers.

S.W.I.N.G. is a set of projects in a city as playground . . . the fun may be of the mind, but its payback must be real. The ideas provide the gentle push that cuts through the still air of division and fears, arcs toward economic benefits, and sweeps back to each new form of creative engagement.

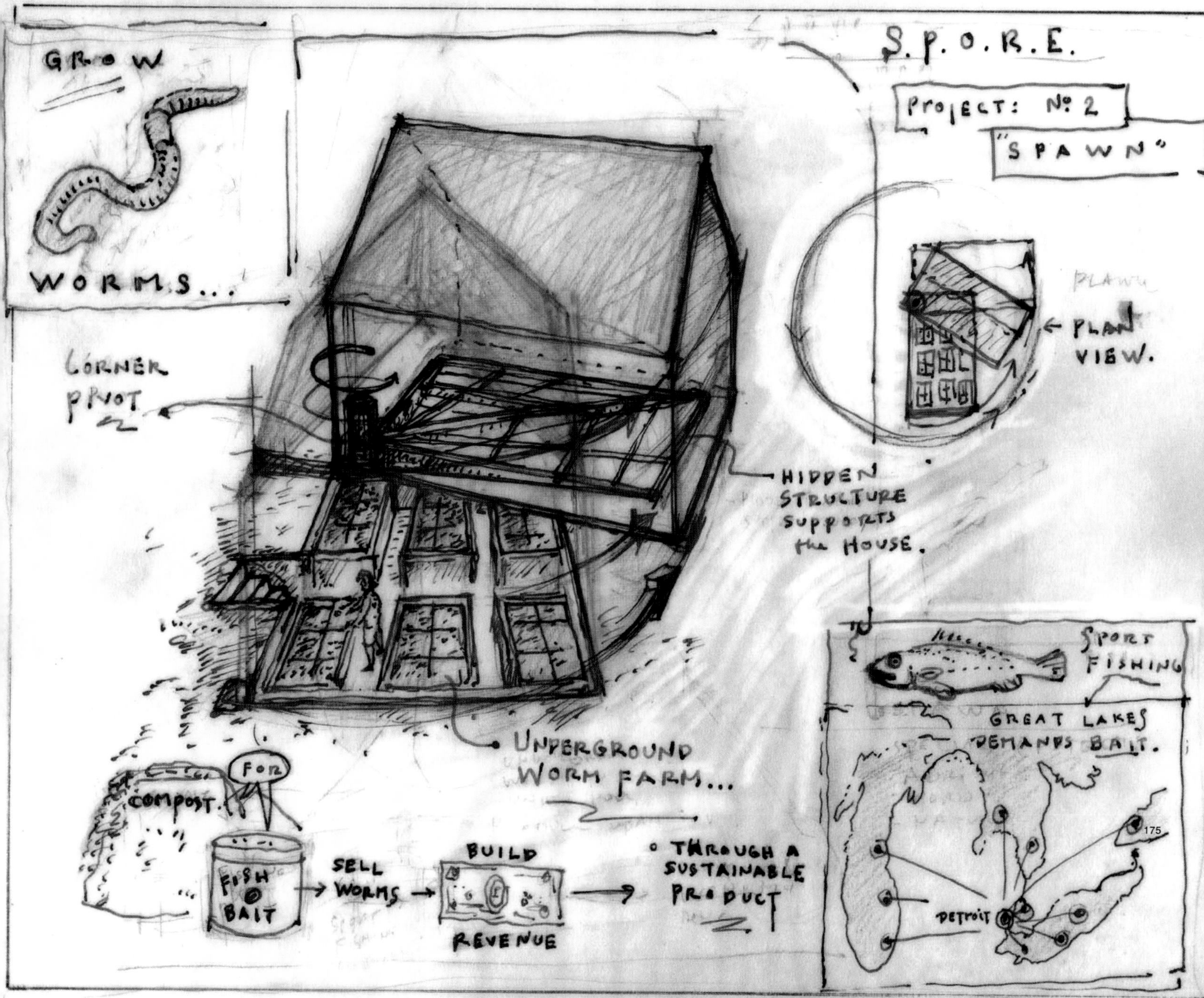
GROW
WORMS...
S.P.O.R.E.
PROJECT: № 2
"SPAWN"
CORNER PIVOT
PLAN VIEW.
HIDDEN STRUCTURE SUPPORTS THE HOUSE.
SPORT FISHING
GREAT LAKES DEMANDS BAIT.
UNDERGROUND WORM FARM...
COMPOST.
FOR
FISH BAIT
SELL WORMS
BUILD
REVENUE
THROUGH A SUSTAINABLE PRODUCT
DETROIT

175

The Urban Ecology of Globalization

Kyong Park/iCUE

Recently, art has projected itself out of studios, galleries, and public spaces into the more complex and meaningful landscapes of economics, politics, and socio-culture. At the same time, the theory and practice of architecture are no longer just about the making of buildings, but have become one of the most engaging subjects of cultural studies.[1] Meanwhile, the fields of geography, anthropology, and sociology are taking a greater interest in architecture and urbanism, recognizing that their works must take on visual and spatial expressions to evolve and be relevant in a world dominated by media-based knowledge constructions. The territories of space and knowledge are increasingly overlapping and multiplying, calling into question the capacity of the Western tradition of dialectical thinking to comprehend and resolve the much more complex and hybrid conditions of contemporary life. The rationalism of the recently completed modernity is no longer the single determinant of the state of society. Perhaps emotions matter as much as physical logic in this world. There are many unanswered old questions and, since the disappearance of the Berlin Wall and the Iron Curtain, there are now new questions about the state of human space.

Disposable Cities

Take Detroit for example. From 1960 to 2000, it lost seventy-five percent of its manufacturing jobs and fifty percent (one million) of its inhabitants and destroyed 200,000 housing units,[2] becoming the largest shrinking city since ancient Rome.[3] The process of deurbanization went something like this. Factories were mothballed under intentional disinvestment and underutilization and machinery was stripped to be sold or moved—often at night to avoid detection from labor unions—while tens of thousands of houses were left abandoned to drive down real estate values and government tax revenues. The result was an increase in taxation of the community; the closing of schools and libraries; a rise in illiteracy, unemployment, and youth gangs; and further isolation of the city and economic dominance by the peripheries. Lending and investing in the city center was fully restricted, creating millions of *tabula rasa* that are ready to be redeveloped at the right time and the right price. The ultimate disposable city, Detroit has been taken over by the ecology of globalization in its first act of massive deurbanization.

1 A decorated bicyclist. Ivanovo, Russia, 2003

2 Wildemere Farms Condos in Macomb Township. Metro Detroit, 2004

3 "Tank," Chris, Kay, "Big-T," "Ben Kids" (left to right) at Cass Avenue and Sproat Street. Detroit, 2004

4 A man who describes himself as "the future CEO of Tycoon Inc," seems to survive by panhandling, often of scaring perspective givers with his menacing stature, amplified by the mystic of black danger, preying on white suburban baseball fans who comes to the new downtown stadium. Detroit, 2004

1

Moving Cities

But Detroit is not simply shrinking; it is also moving, from the point of its origin toward its peripheries. It has been shifting since World War II, after federal policies and programs were put in place to decentralize populations and industries away from urban centers.[4] The most effective motivators were the Federal Housing Act of 1949 that generously insured and lowered mortgages for new houses that were built away from the city, and the Federal Highway Act of 1956 that appropriated $32 billion to construct 41,000 miles of interstate highways so that people could get to homes and jobs that were outside of the city. Cities were asked to move and they did. In Detroit, highways that were ostensibly intended to bring suburbanites to work in the city instead made it possible for people in the city to move out to the suburbs in so-called white flights. It took only roughly fifty years for Detroit to move twenty-five miles out, or about half a mile each year, through a centrifugal process of construction, occupation, abandonment, demolition, and greening.

Sadly, Detroit is not the only moving city.[5] Most cities in the former East Germany are loosing manufacturing jobs and population and are becoming suburbanized.[6] But the consequence there is a spatial segregation and social polarization of different generations, as young families and singles migrate to West Germany, the middle class moves to new single-family houses in the peripheries, and the elderly remain in the old socialist housing blocks.[7] As much as Germany thinks it will never have American ghettos, East Germany nevertheless is being marginalized as a site of active disinvestment and abandonment.[8] As in Detroit, public policy works to convert buildings and cities into green fields, preparing for future redevelopment that will be more realistic and economical than the costly but failed rejuvenation of the East during the euphoria of reunification.[9]

Moving cities, following the vectors of capital dynamics, therefore devour fresh territories and leave non-transformative physical elements such as architecture behind to nature.[10] The physical consequence of this process is the preeminence of infrastructure in the planning and making of the global city,[11] where the city is no longer a place of settlement but rather one of movement. The corporate mergers and conglomeration[12] that coincided with and continued after the deindustrialization of America and other countries enabled the moving of capital from one location to another and from one industry to another. And the rapid movement of capital through the increasingly globalized financial system—"paper entrepreneurialism"[13]—frees funds to go where they can generate profits most rapidly.

Cultural Side Effects from Moving Cities

Ultimately the city, including the suburbs, is a commodity of investment that amortizes in time, and is programmed to die from its inception. In the urban ecology of capitalism, the essence of investment is disinvestment. With the domination of economic space over life space, the city is a resource, and not a place to build the emotional, social, or cultural accumulation of everyday life.

2

5 A gypsy in Skopje, Macedonia. 2005

6 Sudstadt, near Halle, Germany. 2004

7 Friends near Granby Street. Liverpool, 2004

8 A party store at Linwood Avenue and Hazelwood Street, Detroit, 2004

9 An abandoned building functions now as an informal arboretum. Mack Avenue near Lenox Street. Detroit, 2004

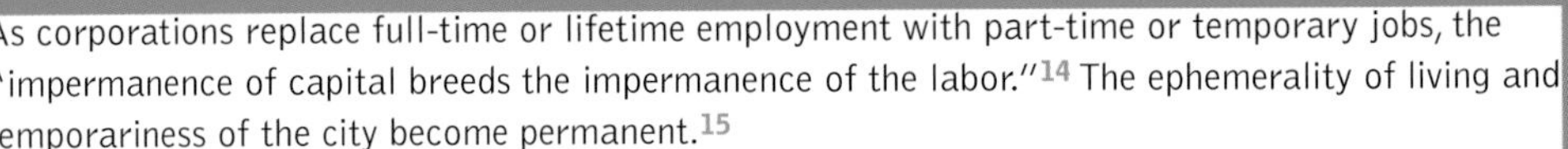

As corporations replace full-time or lifetime employment with part-time or temporary jobs, the "impermanence of capital breeds the impermanence of the labor."[14] The ephemerality of living and temporariness of the city become permanent.[15]

The urban ecology of globalized capitalism also results in a homogenization of the built landscape and the elimination of the distinction between suburban and urban landscapes, specifically through the surburbanization of the city.[16] The conglomeration of the landscape into repetitive and iconic spaces lends a sense of familiarity and comfort, creating a belief and practice that home could be anywhere and everywhere and, therefore, nowhere. The homogenization of the landscape, therefore, complements the movements of capital and labor. Like a malignant cancer, it destroys unique urban cells that are native to particular regions, thus promoting a single type of urban cell that is designed to accommodate homogenized labor and capital.

Globalization of Feudalism

The globalization of capital has zero tolerance for "others"—those who, because of race, gender, or education cannot or do not participate in the incorporation of life—relegating them to dead lands

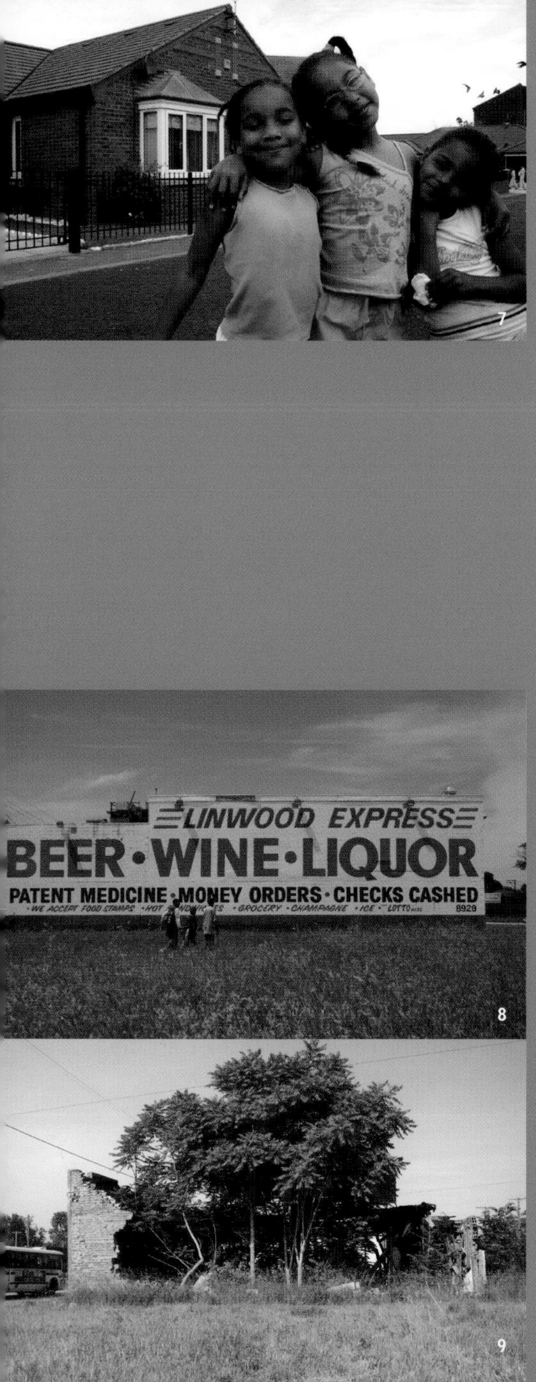

and dead cities. This is disheartening for Germany because it will exclude its own people who have just recently joined the so-called free world. But the process of exclusion through the dismantling of the welfare state and public services is all part of the neo-liberal policies of Western Europe.[17] The process of exclusion recognizes that the unlimited growth model of the free market economy can be sustained only through the exclusion of "others" from social benefits. Although the European Union is expanding rapidly, social reform movements and anti-immigration and anti-refugee policies are also gaining strength in various forms and locations. Nationalism is returning in the midst of supranationalism.

Consequently, the making of a pan-European identity is unexpectedly restoring some of its feudal tradition. As in most American cities, where the majority of the inhabitants moved to the suburbs to pursue the American Dream, leaving a small, marginalized population to live in poverty in the inner cities, Europe is now incarcerating unassimilated foreign-born population in isolated dead lands. By negotiating inclusion and exclusion under the "fiction of a national identity grounded in ethno-cultural homogeneity,"[18] pockets of manageable EU are being constructed within the continent of theoretical EU.[19]

Thus, the age-old Western prejudice against nomadicism is being promoted and re-applied to gypsies and Africans and to the Balkans and former colonies. In the Netherlands, for example, nationalist movements are "openly blaming immigrants [and refugees] for rising crime rates, and seeking to revoke the Schengen Treaty, and close the national borders, and introduce racial quotas for all towns, neighborhoods, and schools, while fervently eager to narrow the Dutch national identity."[20] Expulsions are rising dramatically, and in Germany, refugee families are being returned to their home countries, in the middle of the night with only a few suitcases and Euros.[21]

Soft Borders

Some say the Berlin Wall was built in the wrong place. They proclaim that it should have been at the Polish border instead. But maybe the Wall was never taken down. Instead it just expanded, from Portugal to the Czech Republic, from Cyprus to Sweden. "Not so long ago, any West German who helped an East German over the Wall was a hero. Today, a German helping an illegal Russian into the country must be either an anarchist leftist or a human trafficker."[22]

Fortress Europe is probably the most controversial development project by the EU.[23] Howeover, Turks in Germany and the Netherlands, or Moroccans in Belgium, France, and Italy, are building their own kind of maps—they could perhaps be called the TU or the MU— through communication and trade that territorialize their shared cultural, linguistic, and religious spaces.[24] Strangely, these new maps are reminiscent of the statement "Blood is stronger than a passport" made by a prominent pan-Germanist in 1937, who believed that "the Third Reich had a duty to the whole of the German people, not merely those who happened to live within its current

borders."[25] This idea underlined Hitler's vision of a nation or territorial concept based on race, not on a state.[26]

Thus the border is not an immutable line dedicated to the process of exclusion and inclusion, but rather the frontier of a process in which the movement of population, economy, and information will cause the boundaries, including political ones, to move or falter. The geo-political history of modern Europe affirms that borders move, and are never permanent or impermeable. And, the EU itself is engaged in both moving and open border practices.

Shrinking Nations

Like cities, the founding nation-states of the EU are actually shrinking.[27] From a combination of an increase in life expectancy and a decline in fertility rates, the population of Germany, for instance, is expected to drop from 80 million in 2005 to just 25 million by 2100, and that of Italy from 57.5 million to around 45 million in the same period. This could potentially cause them to fall into an abyss of de-economization that follows depopulation, as happened in most American cities during the post-war period. Unless these nation-states open their borders to younger and more productive foreign-born immigrants, it is possible that the golden era of Western Europe will wind down in the early twenty-first century, due to the cost of maintaining current social and physical infrastructures. At the current demographic trend, for example, only twenty-five percent of the population in the Netherlands will still be Dutch by 2100, raising serious questions about whether ethnicity and culture can remain fixed to a place.

Therefore, the future of the nation-state is not only being challenged by multinational corporations, but also by migrations from economically excluded zones and colonial territories. The latter is a reversed colonization from the territories that had to endure the imposition of the nation-state by European imperialism, a method that extended "the sovereignty of the European nation-states beyond their own boundaries, till nearly all the world's territories were parceled out between themselves."[28] In spite of being further strained by the globalized class struggle in the form of international terror and religious warfare—World War III—the new Europe seems determined to elevate the political and ideological machinery of the nation-state to its own supranational level.

Yet, the delineated territory that intends to efface differences may not survive the transnational demands of the current globalization of labor. Instead the emergence of a new global form of sovereignty with expanding, flexible frontiers that are not tied to the system of modernity requires

10 A Stalinist style apartment building on Rossplatz, Leipzig, Germany, 2004

11 A residential development near Deans gate Station, Manchester, 2004

12 A row of houses, partially occupied, between Belgrade and Novi Sad, Serbia, 2004

13 A village between Ivanovo and Shuya, Russia, 2003

14 Demolished Manchester City Football Club stadium, Manchester, 2004

15 A planned development at West Whitworth Street and Albion Street, near Deans gate Station, Manchester, 2004

16 Informal settlements outside Tirana, Albania, 2005

a "new supranational and de-territorializing regime defined by constant flows of movement (of money, technology, people and goods) along global circuits of production and exchange, in the wake of the demise of the nation state along with the social and political principles."[29]

Globalization from Below: Balkanization

17

To understand the contradiction between the rise of nationalism and the lessening power of the nation-state within the transnationalization of the EU, it may be helpful to examine the process of disintegration of Yugoslavia into micro nation-states that brought similar conflict.[30] First, in the process of fragmentation of its federation, the power and economy of newly formed miniaturized states diminished. The downsizing then extended through the wars and international embargoes of the 1990s. Therefore the emergence of a newly private and informal economy in the ex-Yugoslavia may have become more pixelized and self-enterprising than those of the new nation-states within the ex-Soviet Union. With the state economy and authority greatly reduced and illegitimate, informal urbanism and the black economy, often described as "Wild Cities," spread widely.

The result was a shift in the balance of power between the state and citizen, and the development of informal states made of small-scaled and independent social movements; the pixelation of state down to the family or even the individual. The tiger mapping of Bosnia and Herzegovina through the Dayton Agreement could be considered political confirmation of the general pixelation of the entire society and the downsizing and fragmentation of all forms of entities and their relations throughout the ex-Yugoslavia.

Yet the relations between these disparate entities were more complex than a simple case of divisions. First, informal states became parasitic on the official states using the socialist frameworks for informal practices. Later, the official states participated in and became dependent on the successful informal enterprises of the informal states.[31] A series of parallel or hybrid systems was created in virtually all functions of a society as a nation-state. Neither official nor unofficial states could succeed or survive without a partnership in which the notion of divisions and sovereignties were constantly renegotiated and remade at their soft borders.

Furthermore, new cultural organizations and economic institutions, legal and illegal, were founded through the new and rapid interconnectedness of people and places, often underlined by ethnic, linguistic, cultural and religious identities. Thus the so-called balkanization, or the "globalization from below," began as a counteraction to the exploitative and homogenizing effects of globalization from the ensuing recolonization of the region by adjacent political powers—this time the EU, the United States, and Russia, in a configuration that is reminiscent of the region as a conflict zone between the Ottoman, Hapsburg, and Prussian empires. It is then understandable that the balkanization also offered a sense of independence and freedom to the individuals, families, and institutions that participated in it.

18

Super Localism

While the world was against Serbia—rightfully because of the genocide and ethnic cleansing it conducted in Bosnia and Kosovo—hyper-localism appeared as another form of balkanization. Embodying the sentiment and trauma of a nation fighting against overwhelming international forces, the renegade subculture of Turbo Folk music and mafias thrived, in fairy tale proportions.[32] A mixture of musical celebrities and paramilitary figures rose from the streets or the secret services to capture both illusionary and real resistance against political, military, and cultural forces. Ironically, the resistance took on anti-globalization characteristics—perhaps not so dissimilar to the mystique of Marcos in the Zapatista movement—since the international enemies were also promoting an international market that would later invade and devastate the local economy, particularly the farming region of Vojvodina, the other and lesser known autonomous territory of Serbia.[33] The notion of localism, as a form of self-sufficiency against globalization, seems more effective here than in Detroit, the Sarajevo of the U.S.[34], or in Halle Neustadt, the Detroit of Germany.[35] This suggests the thought that Detroit would have had more success in reconstructing itself if it had been destroyed by actual war and by a discernible enemy from another state.

Therefore, the recent political, cultural, and economic history of the former Yugoslavia is a critical lesson to Europe and to the rest of the world. The experience in this region implies that the borders, identity, and territories of the nation-state are mutable, multiple, and hybrid, and for better or worse, the association of the nation-state with places, history, and culture can be manipulated and adapted in virtually unlimited scale and forms. This is relevant to the future of the EU—and to the rest of the world—as its true and effective democratization will be tested by ethnic, linguistic, cultural, religious, and national identities precisely during the process of constructing a new European identity.

Islands

The federation of Bosnia and Herzegovina is not the only tiger mapping of ethnic or political territories. In the West Bank, settlements are used as militaristic instruments for obtaining

17 Informal settlements in Durres, Albania, 2005

18 Klaus Kretschmann with his girlfriend in Silberhone, near Halle, Germany, 2004

19 A woman with her garden. Ivanovo, Russia, 2003

20 Haverleij, a new development made of collection of castle-like housing blocks in rural area, The Netherlands, 2005

21 Buend Wepner, a shepherd in Sudstadt, near Halle, Germany, 2004

strategic locations intended to lead to a much larger and contiguous take over of the Palestinian territory.[36] And, the split of the United States between its two political parties in the recent presidential election is surprisingly fragmented and complex when the data is examined more closely at different incremental scales and percentages. This reflects the extremely contorted and eclectic shapes of the nation's congressional voting districts through gerrymandering based on education and economic and ethnic conditions.[37] Similarly VINEX, the massive regional housing development of one million units throughout the Netherlands could be a decentralized feudalization of Dutch middle-class communities outside of urban centers, similar to the pixelation of American culture.

Some of these neo-feudal islands are quite explicit, literally fortresses to safeguard territories of higher economy, like the upper middle class housing estates of Haverleij in the Netherlands,[38] the nouveau-riche American-styled communities in China, or the upper-class districts in most Latin American cites. The most blatant and bizarre example of economic islanding is The World in Dubai, the construction and sale of 250 to 300 small, private artificial islands that together form the shape of the world and that you can buy at a starting price of $6.85 million each. However, the biggest economic and cultural island is the United States of America since 9/11, with its federal Department of Homeland Security, although that supremacy is challenged by Fortress Europe.

A Genesis

There is a movement in architecture and urbanism that has been developing outside architecture and urbanism. Starting in the 1980s, the two disciplines were seen as cultural symbols for progress and the future, in the form of controversial corporate icons such as the new AT&T headquarters by Phillip Johnson, the controversial icon of American post-modernist architecture, or large-scale urban developments such as Battery Park City, Canary Wharf and Television City, that entrust to private capitalism the return of economy and culture to the city. Developers such as Olympia and York, Donald Trump, and many others became public celebrities, and the trend of star architects began. The branding of high-designer names, with I.M. Pei, Cesar Pelli and Helmut Jahn leading the way, became linked to the success of developments. Now every city vies

22 An informal settlement outside of Zagreb, Croatia, 2004

to get a Gehry, a Koolhaas, or a Hadid, hoping that the design will free it from the oblivion of de-industrialization. The tiger economies that developed in Asia in the 1990s joined this branding frenzy, as the region's ambitious cities shamelessly imported American and European signature architects and planners to instantly catapult them into the developed economy and culture, they thought.[39]

But the marketing of architects as the agents of globalization has begun to wither. Discontent fueled by exploitation and exclusion ultimately erupted in violent reactions, making the symbols of global capitalism primary and effective targets. The glistening architecture of unabashed capitalism[40] began to disappear from the cover, pages, and screens of mass media. Instead we began to see architecture in destruction, with gaping holes, fallen, or in flames: the burning of the Branch Davidian compound at Waco, Texas; the collapse of the Alfred P. Murrah Federal Building in Oklahoma City; the first attack of the World Trade Center in 1993; the smart bombings of Baghdad, especially in the first Gulf War; the smoldering of the White House (the Russian Parliament building) in Moscow (1993); the destruction of the Parliament building in Sarajevo (1992);[41] and the "terrorist bombing" of numerous American embassies and military buildings in Africa and Middle East. The burning of flags is no longer enough; architecture is the new political effigy, the site and object of violent social reaction.

A Horrible Sensation

The reconstruction of the World Trade Center may be more violent than its destruction. The product of this larger-than-historic event is a diagram of economic and political ambitions, rising on the might of insurance, banking, and state funds. In the eye of this capitalist storm, all involved architects and artists only see the commissions of their lifetimes. The moral ground has been washed away in the redesign of an effigy to be hated.

The opportunity has been lost to find a new form of life, a new construct that did not exist there before, but somehow evolved out of the violence of the event. This millennium may have offered the possibility of a genesis, but instead we chose to bury it, 1776 feet deep.

1 Peter Lang, "Over My Dead City," in *Urban Ecology: Detroit and Beyond*, ed. Kyong Park (Hong Kong: Map Book Publishers, 2005).

2 Coleman Young with Lonnie Wheeler, *Hard Stuff: The Autobiography of Coleman Young* (New York: Viking Adult, 1994), 149.

3 The population of Rome was 1.5 million in 70AD and declined to 30,000 in 7th century in one estimate.

4 In the early years of intercontinental ballistic missiles, nuclear warheads were relatively inaccurate. Therefore, cities became their primary target, which made urban centers a site of potential mass suicide.

5 See Philipp Oswalt, *Atlas of Shrinking Cities* (Berlin: Project Shrinking Cities, 2004).

6 The manufacturing jobs in the chemical industrial zone between Halle—Merseburg—Bitterfeld in East Germany were reduced from 117,000 to 11,000 after the German reunification. At the same time 500,000 single family houses were constructed with massive government subsidies around the peripheries, draining the city and its center, causing more vacancies than the migration to West Germany. Project Shrinking Cities, Berlin 2004

7 The aging and shrinking of the population has enormous negative economic effects, reducing the labor force and forcing them to pay for the increasing number of pensioners. The EU is moving from current 35 to 100 ratio of pensioners to workers to 75 to100 by 2050. The ratio will become one-to-one in Spain and Italy. See Rochus Wiedemer, Why Demolition?: Urban Restructuring of Wolfen-Nord (Berlin: Project Shrinking Cities, 2004). One could easily imagine future economic warfare between the generations, with the elders needing more pension supports while the younger generation is unable to provide more.

8 "350,000 vacant flats will be demolished by the year 2010 as part of the Stadtumbau Ost program [Urban Restructuring of Eastern Germany]" to reduce the surplus of flats in the market. According to Rochus Wiedemer, Why Demolition?: Urban Restructuring of Wolfen-Nord, Project Shrinking Cities, Berlin 2004

9 Germany and the EU have invested more than 1.25 trillion Euros in the reconstruction of East Germany since the reunification.

10 A vast area of Detroit is a countryside now. (See the chapter "Detroit: Making It Better For You" in this book.) With the explosion of the wild pheasant population inside the city, the state of Michigan had embarked on a program to capture them in the city in order repopulate them in the upper peninsula of Michigan that saw a dramatic decline of the pheasant population due to hunting. A few years ago, a deer ran through an empty shop window in downtown Detroit.

11 Forty percent of the land in an average American city is given to freeways, streets, and parking lots. One out of six jobs in the United States is directly or indirectly related to the automobile. Even in the early 1980s, some 10,000 new cars were being added to the roads every 24 hours. See John A. Jackle, *Derelict Landscapes* (Maryland: Rowman and Littlefield Publishers, 1992), 95.

12 "Four or fewer companies dominate 99 percent of the domestic production of cars, 92 percent of the flat glass, 90 percent of cereal breakfast foods, 90 percent of turbines and turbine engines, 90 percent of electric lamps, 85 percent of household refrigerators and freezers, 84 percent of cigarettes, 83 percent of television picture tubes, 79 percent of aluminum productions and 73 percent of tires and inner tubes." Ibid., 85.

13 Dwarfing the trade in manufactured goods, financial markets handles $20 trillion of swaps, options, and other derivatives. Two and a half trillion of foreign currencies are exchanged each day. See Joel Blau, *Illusion of Prosperity: America's Working Families in an Age of Economic Insecurity* (New York: Oxford University Press, 1999), 24.

14 John A. Jackle, *Derelict landscapes* (Maryland: Rowman and Littlefield Publishers, 1992), 75.

15 The Comminssion for a National Agenda for the 1980s, appointed by President Jimmy Carter in 1979, reported that "cities are not permanent" and the policies which treat them as permanent are doomed to fail. Ibid., 78.

16 I think the New Urbanists are really a born-again Anglo Saxon denomination involved in Disney worship. Beyond its religious inspirations, it is more of a real estate practice than an urban planning theory. They hope to be the spiritual leader for the redevelopment of cities that could reap as much financial reward as the building of the suburbs did.

17 In about a fifteen-year period, the Netherlands completely reversed its housing estate by transforming from seventy percent public ownership to seventy percent private ownership nation-wide. From a conversation with Milica Topalovic, Rotterdam, 2005.

18 Fiona Allon, *Boundary Anxieties: Between Borders and Belongings*, Borderlands Ejournal, 2002.

19 Haverleij in the Netherlands may be architecturally the most stunning example of the gated communities in the Fortress Europe. See page 185, photo 20 or http://www.haverleij.nl/index_1.htm.

20 "With each Turkish soccer victory, my hometown suddenly turns into a Little Istanbul, as if we're under temporary foreign occupation." See Herman Asselberghs and Dieter Lesage, *Homo Politicus Pim Fortuyn: A Case Study*, http://www.makeworlds.org/node/38]

21 See *Kenedi Goes Back Home* (*Kenedi se vraca kuci*), 2003. A film by Zelimir Zilnik, 74 min.

22 See Herman Asselberghs and Dieter Lesage, *Homo Politicus Pim Fortuyn: A Case Study*, http://www.makeworlds.org/node/38]

23 See Zelimir Zilnik, *Fortress Europe* (*Trdnjava Evropa*) 2000. A film by Zelimir Zilnik, 80 min.

24 Ivan Nio, "Ethnoscape," in *Euroscape*, Ivan Nio, et al (Amsterdam: Must Publishers, 2003), 93.

25 Mark Mazower, *Dark Continent* (New York: Vintage, 1998), 70.

26 Ibid.

27 Worker Longer and Live Longer, *The Economist*, September, 27, 2003, Vol.368, 13.

28 Fiona Allon, *Boundary Anxieties: Between Borders and Belongings*, Borderlands Ejournal, 2002.

29 M. Hardt and A. Negri, *Empire* (Cambridge: Harvard University Press, 2000).

30 Its important to note that Yugoslavia was in-between and separate state, both politically and economically, from the dual parity of communist and capitalist blocks.

31 One of many examples, the traffic authority of Belgrade participated in informal economy by selling semi-official permits to 'wild kiosk' owners on, for instance' on the parking lots on which they had authority upon, thereby supplementing their meager salaries. See Dzokic, Kucina, Neelen and Topalovic, "Belgrade: Fragments for Wild City," in *Beograd-Den Haag* (The Hague: Stroom, 2003).

32 The wedding of "Zaliko Raznatovic—Arkan, the long career gangster with the high ranking position in communist police/secret service, owner of a pastry shop and businessman, collctor of art, boss of the soccer team supporters, convicted war criminal, member of the Parliament and national hero [killed on in the lobby of Belgrade Intercontinental Hotel] and his wedding with Svetlana Velickovic, the ultimate star of Serbian turbo-folk music, whom he kidnapped, was the event of the year." See Mileta Prodanovic, in *Beograd-Den Haag* (The Hague: Stroom, 2003).

33 The sentiment to international forces are more positive in Kosovo, as they are seen as the savior from the oppression of the Kosovo independence movements from Serbian rule that dates back hundereds of years. Bill Clinton Street and Bob Dole Avenue makes an intersect in Prishtina, the capital of Kosovo.

34 Detroit, with 82 percent of its population being black and 81% of its suburban population being white, would qualify as a case of ethnic cleansing that has been associated with Sarajevo.

35 Halle Neustadt, in 35% depopulation since the re-unification, at the start of the demolition of 26 large high-rise housing blocks, and economically depended on massive state subsidy, parallels the urban condition of Detroit.

36 See Anselm Franke, Eyal Weizman, *Territories: Islands, Camps and Other States of Utopia* (Berlin: Verlag Der Buchhandlung Walther Konig, 2003).

37 Ibid. and http://www-personal.umich.edu/~mejn/election/, http://www.princeton.edu/~rvdb/JAVA/election2004/

38 http://www.haverleij.nl/index_1.htm

39 See Kyong Park, "Images of the Future: The Architecture of a New Geography," in *Unmapping the Earth* (Kwangju: 97 Kwangju Biennale, 1997), 124-143.

40 Michael Douglass, "Greed is good," in the film *Wall Street*, Oliver Stone, 1987.

41 See photos 1 and 2 on page 10 of this book.

42 Larry A. Silverstein may be the luckiest man of the 21st century so far. After acquiring a 99 year lease on the WTC just six weeks before the 9/11, this aging complex would have surely needed redevelopment soon to stay competitive in the office rental market. Well, he got a free demolition, insurance money and state supports, so that he could rebuilt the site into a highly symbolic and profitable development.

Architecture of Resistance
Urban Workshop
Near eastside, Detroit
1999

Participating Artists and Architects
Mark Anderson (Seattle)
Mel Chin/Linda Larsen (North Carolina)
Renee Greene (New York)
Rick Lowe (Houston)
Peter Lynch (Detroit)
Deborah Grotfledt (Houston)
Tricia Ward (Los Angeles)
Michael Sorkin/Andrej Vovk (New York)
Meg Webster (New York)
Tyree Guyton/Jenenne Whitfield (Detroit)
Andrew Zago (Detroit)
Janine Debonne (Detroit)
Stephen Vogel (Detroit)
Hannes Brunner (Germany)
Doran Gill (London)

Staff
Architecture Coordination Peter Magoulick
Childrens' Workshops Dada Flounory
Graphic and Web Page Design Craig Bachellier

Workshop Participants
Trevor Behner (Detroit)
Abir Ali (Detroit)
Susanne Koehler (Germany)
Isabel Becker (Germany)
Clemens Austen (Germany)
Marcos van Steekelenburg (The Netherlands)
Ian Young (University of Pennsylvania)
Mark Gardner (University of Pennsylvania)
Will Hentschel (University of Pennsylvania)
Julie Moskovitz (University of Pennsylvania)

Special thanks to: Grace Lee Boggs, Lee Burns, Steven Demeter, Gerald Hairston, Shea Howell, Ashley Kyber, Greg Siwak, Joe Weertz, Gabriel Weertz, Nkenge Zola

In collaboration with
Detroit Summer Youth Program
Project Rowe House Foundation (Houston)
The Heiderberg Project (Detroit)
Arts Corp (Los Angeles)
LifeLand (Detroit)

Detroit: Making It Better for You (A Fiction)
Video
09.28 Minutes
2000

Video Editing/Composition Joshua Pearson

Videography
Kyong Park
Kiersten Armstrong
G. Todd Roberts
Allegra Pitera

Screenplay Kyong Park
Editor Joshua Pearson
Narrator Joshua Pearson

Soundtrack
Warmfuzzy Jason Hogans
Esteem Jason Hogans
Landscaping Recloose
Dencity Recloose
All courtesy of Carl Craig and Planet-E

Director Kyong Park

Advisors
Stephen P. Vogel
Daniel Pitera

Research Greg Siwak

Assistants
Graig Donnelly
Andrew Sturm

Transportation Rebecca Donnelly-Hitch

Thanks to: Grace Lee Boggs, Tyree Guyton,, David Hacker, Gerald Hairston, Peter Magoulic, Kelly Powell, Barbara Rennie, Brenda Smith, Anita Vogel, Paul Weertz, Jennene Whitfield, Nkenge Zola

24260: The Fugitive House
Traveling House: 20 side wall panels, 12 front wall panels, and 11 floor sections
13,100 kg
26′ 3″ x 20′ 4″ x 25′ 9″

1
Detroit, USA (circa 1920–2001)

In collaboration with Daniel Pitera/DCDC/UDM

Project Coordinator Andrew Sturm

Video Documentation
Allegra Pitera
Kyong Park

Project Team
Saad al-Ajemi
Graig Donnelly
Jason Fowler
Manny Garza
Matt Gerard
Andrew Lehman
Jessica Schulte
Mike Spencer

Special Advisors
Chris Turner
Sean Sruger

Technical Advisors
Matt Tatarian
Greg Jackunis

2
Orléans, France
3rd annual Archilab exhibition/conference (May 11-June 30, 2001)

Curators
Béatrice Simonet
Marie-Ange Brayer

Project Coordinator Andrew Sturm

Project Team (Detroit)
Graig Donnelly
Jason Fowler,
Manny Garza
Matt Gerard
Andrew Lehman,
Jessica Schulte
Mike Spencer

Project Team (Orléans)
Florent Radiguet
Nicolas Gauthier
Alexander Temlier,
Peggy Housset
Elise Novak
Clemence Monnet
Pierre Brissonet

3
Sindelfingen, Germany (2001)
One Site/Two Places

Organized by
Kunst & Projekte
Galerie der Stadt Sindelfingen

Curators Ingrid and Konrad Burgbacher

24260 Soundtrack Text Kyong Park
Narrator Anne Peters
Sound Engineer and Editor Benno Peters

Thanks to Institute für Phonetik und Digitale in Universität Kiel

4
Den Haag
WAYS OUT at Stroom (February 6–April 27, 2002)
Stored (2002-04)

Curators
Jan Wijle
Lily van Ginneken

Project Coordinator Marc Claejis

5
Hamburg, Germany
Art & Economy at Deichtorhallen (February 28–June 23, 2002)

6
Karlsruhe, Germany
PARA > SITES: Who is moving the global city? (January 28–March 30, 2003)

Badischer Kunstverein [WHAT IS THIS?]
Curator Angelika Stepken

7
Dessau, Germany
Stored (2003–05) [MOVED DATE FOR CONSISTENCY]

8
Sheffield, UK (October–November, 2004)

Project Team
Mark Broom
Stuart Curran
Jonathan Drage
Vanessa Peace
Kay Robson
Neil Sansom
Ruth Sienkiewicz
Vicky Stoddard
Jon Wallis
SimonWatkins
Carolyn Butterworth

Project Manager Malcolm Fielding

Sponsors
Sheffield City Council
The Cultural Industries Quarter Agency
Arts Council England
J.W. Northend Ltd.
The Yorkshire, London, UK

9
Leipzig, Germany
Project Shrinking Cities (September, 2005)

Words, Images, and Spaces:
A Language for a New City?
Workshop, installations, and video
Near eastside, Detroit
2002

Project Director Kyong Park

Project Team
Francisca Benitez
Anthony Hamboussi
Toni Moceri
Pilar Ortiz
Manuela Tromben
Tony King

Videographers
Francisca Benitez
Pilar Ortiz
Kyong Park

Photographers
Anthony Hamboussi
Kyong Park
G. Todd Roberts

Thanks to: Brian du Bois, Najahyia Chinchilla, Joe Frye, John Havranek, Jeff Havranek, Carrie Havranek, Chris Turner

Video soundtracks courtesy of Carl Craig and Planet-E

Video Editor Manuela Tromben

The above projects were sponsored by Detroit Collaborative Design Center/University of Detroit Mercy

In collaboration with Home: Made in Detroit, a program of StoreFront for Art and Architecture

Funded by
McMartha Fund
The Rockefeller Foundation
Andy Warhol Foundation
Stephen A. and Diana L. Goldberg Foundation
The National Endowment for the Arts

Architecture of Resistance was also funded by
Cultural Foundation of Thurgau County (Switzerland)
Cultural Foundation of the Federal Government of Switzerland
Pro Helvetia Cultural Foundation (Switzerland)
National Planning Board (The Netherlands)
Univeristy of Pennsylvania (School of Architecture)
Ghafari Associates (Detroit)

The Slide
Video
03.27 minutes
Halle Neustadt, Germany
2003

Assistant and 3-D Computer Modeling Marco Braun
Video Editor Christian Betz
Graphic Design and Photo Imaging Sabine Horlitz
Photo Imaging Armin Schmidt
Consultant Engineer Martin Strewinski

Actors
The mayor of Halle Neustadt Bert Pepert
A teenager Florian Tieseler
A young woman 2 Carolin Ernst
An urban planner Ute Lindenbeck
A young woman 1 Anna Kohlmeier
A mother Brigitte Ronne

Thanks to: Benjamin Foerster-Baldenius, Cora Hegewald, Matthias Rick

Commissioned and presented at the project Hotel Neustadt, published as: Thalia Theatre Halle (ed.), *Hotel Neustadt*, Berlin, Alexander Verlag Berlin, 2004

Funded by Kulturstiftung des Bundes, German Federal Cultural Foundation (among others)

BAR/GDR/FRG (BRQ/DDR/BRD):
A Very Slow Look at the Three Cities in Dresden
Video installation
18.38 minutes
Dresden, Germany
2003

Director Kyong Park
Video Editor Thilo Fröbel
Sound Editor Torsten Birne
Camera 1 Johannes Köhler
Camera 2 Thilo Fröbel
Camera 3 Kyong Park

Thanks to: Torsten Birne, Christiane Mennicke, Christoph Bohsen, Harald Schlüttig/SAEK, Susanne Altmann, Sophie Goltz, Eugene Goltz, Paul Elsner, Florian Trüstedt, Ulrich Gärtner, MDR

Translator Juliane Kaul

Narrative Source
Ingolf Rossberg Politician, former head of the Planning Department and current mayor of Dresden
Wolfgang Kil Architect/Critic
Hermann Krüger Department of Historic Preservation, Dresden
Gerhard Glaser Department of Historic Preservation, State of Saxony
Wolfgang Schürmann Architect
Kurt Biedenkopf Former Prime Minister of the State of Saxony

The recordings were produced from Wolfram Nagel (1994–1997)

Commissioned by and presented in Dresden Postplatz: Public Sampler

Concept Torsten Birne

Organization
Torsten Birne
Sophie Goltz
Paul Elsner

Funded by the Kulturstiftung des Bundes (among others)

OldHouseNewHouse/NewCityOldCity
Video
36.01 minutes
Metro Detroit
2004

Video and Audio Editors
Garret Linn
Manuela Tromben

Videography
Kyong Park
Manuela Tromben

Photography
Kyong Park
Manuela Tromben

Subtitles and Titles Garret Linn
Translator Peter Friedrich

Associate Producer Jim Cope
Director Kyong Park

Interviewees
Ronnie Bennierfield
Charles Blackburn
Virginia Cantrell
Lorenzo and Dora Castillo
Cassandra and Larry Caulford
Scott and Michelle Cope
Mario Faccioni
Gary Garrett
John George
Jeff Jenks
Audra Kubats
Jane and Randy Lynn
Mickey Nemer
Toni Moceri
Ralph Taylor
Rudy Williams

Thanks to Mitch Cope

Commissioned by and presented in Project Shrinking Cities
A project of the Kulturstiftung des Bundes

CityMix
Video
36.01 minutes
Metro Detroit; Halle/Leipzig, Germany; Ivanovo, Russia; Liverpool/Manchester, UK
2004

Video Editor Garret Linn
Videography Kyong Park
Photography Kyong Park

Director Kyong Park

Thanks to: James Bolchover, Joshua Bolchover, Paul Domela, Severine Domela, Jens Fischer, Leo Fitzmaurice, Jean Grant, Katja Heinecke , Annie Janusch , Robert McDonald, Anne König, Imogen Stidworthy, Ben Perry, Sofie Thorsen , Blanka Stolz, Rochus Wiedemer, Dominic Wilkinson, Tobias Zielony

Commissioned by Project Shrinking Cities
A project of the Kulturstiftung des Bundes, German Federal Cultural Foundation

Halle-Neustadt, Germany. 2004